THE
HEALING
HANDBOOK

DESTINY IMAGE BOOKS BY KYNAN BRIDGES

Possessing Your Healing

Supernatural Favor

90 Days to Possessing Your Healing

The Power of Unlimited Faith

THE

an essential guide

HEALING

to healing the sick

HANDBOOK

kynan bridges

DESTINY IMAGE® PUBLISHERS, INC.
P.O. Box 310, Shippensburg, PA 17257-0310
"Promoting Inspired Lives."

This book and all other Destiny Image and Destiny Image Fiction books are available at Christian bookstores and distributors worldwide.

Cover design by: Prodigy Pixel

For more information on foreign distributors, call 717-532-3040.
Reach us on the Internet: www.destinyimage.com.

ISBN 13 TP: 978-0-7684-0667-2
ISBN 13 eBook: 978-0-7684-0668-9

For Worldwide Distribution, Printed in the U.S.A.
1 2 3 4 5 6 7 8 / 19 18 17 16 15

CONTENTS

CHAPTER 1

THE GARDEN OF EDEN: GOD'S BLUEPRINT

Let us make man in our image, after our likeness: and let them have dominion over the fish of the sea, and over the fowl of the air, and over the cattle, and over all the earth, and over every creeping thing that creepeth upon the earth (Genesis 1:26).

On October 1, 1908, Ford Motor Company released their famous Ford Model T. This was one of the first and most popular gasoline automobiles of its kind. Prior to this time, cars were not affordable for the average consumer. Beyond affordability was the issue of availability. In fact, the whole goal for building the Model T was to make cars readily available for the masses. In the words of Henry Ford himself:

> I will build a car for the great multitude. It will be large enough for the family but small enough for the individual to run and care for. It will be

constructed of the best materials, by the best men to be hired, after the simplest designs that modern engineering can devise. But it will be so low in price that no man making a good salary will be unable to own one—and enjoy with his family the blessing of hours of pleasure in God's great open spaces.[1]

In many ways, Ford was a pioneering engineer—an architect. Henry Ford's design became a blueprint or model for American cars. The Model T would set forth the outline of all Ford vehicles thereafter, which would be mass-produced on an assembly line (another method pioneered by Ford). This was a design that many manufacturers would follow even until today.

GOD'S ORIGINAL BLUEPRINT

In the book of Genesis, God revealed His original blueprint for us as His creation; He called them Adam and Eve. By *blueprint* we are referring to a design plan or model. Like the Model T, Adam and Eve served as the original design for all of humanity. God took the best materials and created man in His very own image. The Bible says, "Let us make man in our image, after our likeness: and let them have dominion" (Gen. 1:26). What does this dominion look like and what does the issue of dominion have to do with divine healing?

The word *dominion* comes from the Hebrew word *radah*, which means to rule, dominate, or subjugate. The purpose of God was to be carried out in the earth by humankind.

We were commissioned to expand the dominion of God throughout the entire planet. Adam and Eve were never sick, lonely, impoverished, afraid, or insecure. Everything on the earth was to be subject to them. In fact, they were in perfect fellowship with God. They walked in the Garden of God in the cool of the day without the slightest sense of guilt or shame. The Bible says:

> *And God blessed them, and God said unto them, Be fruitful, and multiply, and replenish the earth, and subdue it: and have dominion over the fish of the sea, and over the fowl of the air, and over every living thing that moveth upon the earth* (Genesis 1:28).

The word *fruitful* comes from the Hebrew word *parah* which means to "branch off." God intended for the people He created to grow, multiply, and expand across the earth. Through this process of dominion and multiplication, the entire earth would have been populated with a perfect homogeneous race of men and women, created in the flawless image of God Himself. This spiritual blueprint would serve as the design standard for all of creation.

However, there was a problem. This problem was called sin. In Genesis chapter 3, Eve was tempted by the serpent (Satan) and seduced into partaking of the Tree of the Knowledge of Good and Evil. She ate from the tree and gave to Adam, and he also ate (see Gen. 3:6). The moment they ate from this tree, they fell from perfect fellowship and communion with God. The moment they rebelled against

God in such a way, they died. In other words, they were separated from God in spirit, soul, and body. This is how sin and sickness came into the world as we know it. This sin corrupted God's blueprint for humankind.

Prior to this fall, Adam and Eve were destined to live a life of divine health, soundness of mind, never-ending joy, and everlasting life. Now, as a result of the death ushered in through Adam and Eve, we live in a fallen world. People get sick, experience chronic ailments, and ultimately die prematurely as a result of the curse of sin. What was the solution to this fallen state? The efficacious sacrifice of Jesus on the cross became the only means by which the curse of sin could be broken. Contrary to popular belief, sickness was never in God's original design. He never intended for us to be sick. It was never God's agenda for people to be bound with cancer, diabetes, lupus, multiple sclerosis, and other chronic conditions. We were destined to reign on the earth and live forever. Isn't that an amazing reality?

DIVINE HEALTH: MAN'S INHERITANCE

Like any blueprint, the creation account found in Genesis gives us a deeper understanding of the way things should be. Every manufacturer has a blueprint that they follow in order to ensure efficiency and consistency in process. In this regard, God is no different. If we want to understand God's will for mankind (especially as it relates to healing), we need to look to creation. This was the spiritual precedent or blueprint. He had a specific purpose in mind when He created Adam and Eve; this purpose was to take dominion in the earth. What was the implication of man's creation? One aspect that we can't ignore is the reality that Adam was never sick. He was in perfect health. This is what we call divine health (which we will discuss in much detail later).

Adam and Eve never had to visit a doctor or have surgery, or take prescription medication—there were no doctors or hospitals anyway, of course. They were completely oblivious to the notion of cancer, heart disease, infirmity, or even death for that matter. This was God's gift to His new creation. It was not just a haphazard quality, but it was an intentional expression of God's goodness toward humankind. Just as God Himself was never sick, man was ordained to enjoy the same quality of life that God has in Himself. Man was actually made in the divine image of God, which implies that the very DNA of God was in Adam. The Bible says, "And the Lord God formed man of the dust of the ground, and breathed into his nostrils the breath of life; and man became a living soul" (Gen. 2:7). The word *breath* comes from the Hebrew *nĕshamah*, which means "spirit." God literally breathed His very Spirit into man. Through this divine process man became a "living soul" or "living and active being." As a result of the indwelling of God's spirit, man possessed eternal life.

Earlier we introduced the concept of sin and its effects on humanity as a whole. Sin perverted humankind's inheritance of perfection into an inheritance of dysfunction and corruption. In fact, sickness is simply the dysfunction of the body as a result of original sin. That which was designed to be a blessing became a curse. Through man's transgression, he came out from God's canopy of blessing and protection and became subject to the very elements that God gave him dominion over. Remember, Adam and Eve were to exercise dominion in the earth. Once they sinned, this divine order was reversed—the earth began to exercise dominion over them. This truth is illustrated in Genesis 3:17:

> *And unto Adam he said, Because thou hast hearkened unto the voice of thy wife, and hast eaten of the tree, of which I commanded thee, saying, Thou shalt not eat of it: cursed is the ground for thy sake; in sorrow shalt thou eat of it all the days of thy life.*

Notice that God told Adam that the ground was cursed for his sake, and that he would eat from it in sorrow all the days of his life. The word *sorrow* comes from the Hebrew word `*itstsabown*, which means pain, labor, hardship, sorrow, or toil (Strong's, H6087). The very ground that God commanded to yield forth its fruit to Adam became a source of pain, hardship, and toil. Also, we see that now Adam had a definitive life span. That is to say, he had an expiration date. All of these factors were brought into being through the curse.

HUMANKIND'S THREE-PART DEATH

Unfortunately, Adam and Eve's transgression didn't only affect their individual condition, but their sin affected all of humanity. This is one of the reasons why men and women are in a state of rebellion against God this very day. Adam and Eve possessed a tripartite nature. In other words, we as human beings consist of spirit, soul, and body. Man's sin affected all three aspects of his existence. When God told Adam, "You shall surely die," He wasn't just talking about physical death, but He was referring to the death of the spirit and soul as well. As a result of eating from the Tree of the Knowledge of Good and Evil, the entire human race was separated from intimate fellowship with God. This was the first aspect of man's death. This is what we call the death of the spirit or spiritual death. Through the sin of our original grandparents, shame, guilt, and condemnation were ushered in, as well as the consciousness of good and evil. Before sin, Adam was completely ignorant of evil and the need to cover his sin through self-effort. The moment he bit from the fruit, his spirit man died, and he was aware of his own insufficiency and incompleteness. In this very moment, man became enslaved to a sinful nature.

DEATH OF THE SOUL

The second aspect of man's death was that of the soul. The soul is the seat of the mind, will, and emotions. Adam and Eve not only lost their spiritual connection with God, but they also lost their peace. Through their rebellion, Adam and Eve opened their mind to sin consciousness. By sin consciousness, I am referring to the preoccupation with sin as a barrier between God and man. This barrier causes man to perform for God's love and acceptance. It also causes man to be subjected to fear, worry, shame, guilt, doubt, and bitterness. Adam and Eve were brought into bondage to the spirit and the emotion of fear. For the first time in human-kind's existence, they felt a sense of anxiety.

And they heard the voice of the Lord God walking in the garden in the cool of the day: and Adam and his wife hid themselves from the presence of the Lord God amongst the trees of the garden (Genesis 3:8).

Adam and Eve were terrified of God. They were afraid of the consequences of their sin; this is the manifestation of the death of the soul. In fact, the word for "hid" is the Hebrew word chaba' and it means to "withdraw oneself" or "to be forced into hiding" (Strong's, H2245). Human-kind was withdrawn from God's presence and thrust into a mental and emotional state of chaos. Talk about serious consequences to sin!

PHYSICAL DEATH

As a result of the fall, humankind was ultimately sub-jected to physical death. Adam and Eve would no longer live forever. This death also includes the proliferation of sick-ness, because man would eventually undergo the failure of vital organs in his body, causing death. Although, living for nearly a thousand years wasn't too bad! This dimension of man's death is the primary reason why we must war against sickness and disease in this generation.

We will deal with all three aspects of man's fall, but the bulk of our discussion will be on physical and emotional healing in this book. God wants to restore humanity to His original design for us. He wants us to experience the blessings and benefits of fellowship with Him—namely, divine health and healing. Though we cannot completely eradicate sickness in this fallen world as a whole (sickness will ultimately be done away with in heaven), we can be healthy and whole while we are here on planet earth so that we can fulfill the great commission (see Matt. 28:19). Jesus Christ came and died on the cross to reverse the curse brought upon humankind through Adam's transgression. Through His blood (which we will talk about in a later chapter) we have been released from the bondage of sin and its effects—sickness, poverty, and death.

Through the pages of this book you will learn the practical yet powerful keys to healing the sick and walking in divine health. It doesn't matter whether you are a pastor, layman, or businessperson; you can heal the sick. The reason I know this is because Jesus said you could!

SUMMARY QUESTIONS

1. What was God's original design for His creation?

2. What is meant by the term *dominion?*

3. What does humankind's call to dominion have to do with divine healing?

4. What were the three areas of man's death?

NOTE

1. Henry Ford and Samuel Crowther, *My Life and Work* (Garden City, NY: Doubleday, Page &, 1922), 73.

CHAPTER 2

HEALING DEFINED

If thou wilt diligently hearken to the voice of the Lord thy God, and wilt do that which is right in his sight, and wilt give ear to his commandments, and keep all his statutes, I will put none of these diseases upon thee, which I have brought upon the Egyptians: for I am the Lord that healeth thee (Exodus 15:26).

God desires for you to be healed. He desires for you to heal the sick! The question remains: what is divine healing? Simply put, divine healing is the manifestation of health and wholeness in the spirit, soul, and/or body of a person. The Bible uses the Hebrew word *rapha* which means "to heal" or "to make healthful" (Strong's, H7495). The word also means "Physician." In Exodus 15, the children of Israel came to the waters of Marah. These waters were extremely "bitter" or contaminated. As the people cried out to Moses, God showed him a tree to throw into the waters. Once he obeyed God's instruction, the waters became sweet. In this scenario God revealed Himself to the Israelites as "Jehovah Rapha" or "Jehovah Ropheka" which means "The Great Physician." This was God's first personal revelation to the Israelites after their captivity in Egypt for 430 years.

We see, then, that healing is not just something God does, but healing is God's nature. God is the Healer! This is the basis for our approach to the subject of healing. In fact, God longs to heal you! He deeply desires to manifest Himself to the people you care about. Notice that God did not reveal Himself to the Israelites as a God of destruction or death. Before they ever received the Ten Commandments, God show them that He is the Healer. Hallelujah!

WHY HEALING?

Why is the subject of healing so important? Simply put, healing is the divine inheritance of every born-again believer. Jesus Christ paid a tremendous price for our healing (which we will discuss in further detail in a later chapter). Furthermore, there is an epidemic of sickness in the body of Christ. Satan is afflicting the people of God with so much sickness and disease that many in the church have lost hope in the prospect of ever being healed. Others have blamed God as unfair and unfaithful. Nothing could be further from the truth. God is faithful and just! Sickness was never a part of His original plan in the earth.

Before we can experience divine healing or minister healing to others, we must realize the true nature of God as revealed in His Word. We must also realize the necessity for healing in the earth today. In my years of ministry,

I have seen God perform miraculous healings in people's lives including terminal cancer being healed, multiple sclerosis being healed, limbs growing out, tumors dissolving instantly, lame people walking, and metal turning into bone (just to name a few examples). The question is: are these haphazard or random occurrences, or can we all tap in to God's healing power on a regular basis? I want to submit to you (based on the authority of Scripture) that divine healing belongs to you. Through the authority of God's Word and the power of the Holy Spirit, you can heal the sick. Healing can become a consistent reality in your life.

Healing is the divine inheritance of every believer, bought with the precious blood of Jesus.

There is an intrinsic desire for people to be healthy and whole. In fact, there has been a resurgence of New Age healing practices in the Western world. People are choosing to seek healing outside of the traditional confines of modern medicine. Instead, many are opting for acupuncture, energy healing, shamanic healing, and other occult practices. Why? I believe people are desperate for solutions to the problem of sickness and disease, which are not found in our current healthcare system. Instead of coming to Christ for healing, people are relying on their own fallen humanity to produce healing in their lives. This is very unfortunate, because the church holds the answer to the problem of sickness in the world—Jesus Christ. Even more tragic is the reality that a large percentage of the church does not believe in divine healing at all. In my opinion, any pastor who doesn't teach his flock about God's promise of healing and wholeness needs to find another vocation. Due to the lack of healing power available in most churches, the world is unknowingly (and sometimes knowingly) going to Satan to heal them. How ironic is this? People are consulting demonic power— the same demonic power that made them sick in the first place—to experience healing. This is not the will of God, beloved! He wants all of us to experience healing in our total person.

THE CHILDREN'S BREAD

But Jesus said unto her, Let the children first be filled: for it is not meet to take the children's bread, and to cast it unto the dogs (Mark 7:27).

Contrary to popular belief, divine healing is not just something that God "might do" if it is His will. That is, healing is not an occasional or spontaneously occurring act that takes place without our knowledge, faith, or participation. I am not saying that God can't heal any way He wants; He definitely can! I am simply saying that the plan of God to heal the sick is a clear biblical reality. It is the will of God to heal the sick, plain and simple!

In Mark 7, a Syrophoenician woman requesting that He cast an unclean spirit out of her daughter approached

Jesus. This woman was in a very desperate situation. Instead of responding with compassion and understanding, Jesus said this: "Let the children first be filled: for it is not meet to take the children's bread, and to cast it unto the dogs" (Mark 7:27).

This was definitely not a "politically correct" statement. The use of the word *dog* was a cultural misnomer alluding to the fact that she was a Gentile. Not only was she Gentile, she was a Syrophoenician. The Jews of that era had a special hatred for Syrophoenicians. Instead of walking away despondent or rejected, the woman responded by saying: "Yes, Lord: yet the dogs under the table eat of the children's crumbs" (Mark 7:28). Jesus marveled at her words! "And he said unto her, For this saying go thy way; the devil is gone out of thy daughter" (Mark 7:29).

This woman received her miracle. Notice that she never refuted any of Jesus's statements. She never once became offended. All she did was believe, and as a result she tapped in to the covenant of healing. Why do I use the term "covenant of healing"? Jesus referred to something called "the children's bread." What was He talking about? He used the Greek word *teknon* (Strong's, G5043), meaning "offspring" or "my child." This was a term of affection or endearment. It was a term God used exclusively to describe the people of Israel as the "apple of His eye." In other words, it is the responsibility of the father to supply the needs of His children, especially those closest to His heart. It is a covenant right. Simply put, healing is a divine right or covenant that God has made with His children. Even though this woman was not an Israelite, she still partook of "the children's bread" by faith. How much more do those of us who have a relationship with God have a right to divine healing?

A DIVINE RIGHT

When you think of something that is a right, what comes to mind? A right is defined as a moral or legal entitlement to have or obtain something or to act in a certain way. Based on this definition and the reference made to healing being "the children's bread," we know that healing is something we are entitled to. Many people do not know (or do not believe) they are entitled to healing. The moment you became born again (i.e. accept Jesus Christ as Lord by faith) you became a child of God entitled to all the rights and privileges as a naturally born son or daughter. Do you realize that God is your Father? Have you considered the enormous implications of such a profound truth? In fact, Jesus said:

> For every one that asketh receiveth; and he that
> seeketh findeth; and to him that knocketh it shall
> be opened. Or what man is there of you, whom if
> his son ask bread, will he give him a stone? Or if
> he ask a fish, will he give him a serpent? If ye then,
> being evil, know how to give good gifts unto your
> children, how much more shall your Father which
> is in heaven give good things to them that ask him?
> (Matthew 7:8-11)

Notice that Jesus makes a stark comparison between earthly parents and the Father. If fallible man, being evil, knows how to give good gifts to his physical children, how much more will God give good gifts to His spiritual children? This is a rhetorical question designed to cause us to consider the good nature of God. I don't know any parent who wouldn't do everything in their power to make their child well if they were sick. Why then do we think that God doesn't want us to be healed and whole? God absolutely wants us to be in health. In fact, He paid a tremendous price for our healing (which we will talk about later). Healing is more than just a favor God extends; it is the right of us, His children.

You may be reading this book thinking, "I didn't know I had a right to be healed!" Well, now you do! You don't have to beg and plead for healing; all you need to do is know your rights! Not only do you have a right to be healed, but you have been given the right to heal others. Once you embrace your identity as a child of God, you will soon realize that healing is much easier than you think! Receive "the children's bread" today!

HEALING TESTIMONY

There was a young lady in our church who came to the altar for healing. She was dealing with some chromosomal anomalies since her birth. While praying for her, I prophesied that she would heal the sick. She believed the word that I spoke over her life with all her heart.

Shortly after, this same young lady walked into a cancer ward and prayed for a man who was diagnosed with end-stage cancer. The doctors gave him three to six months to live. She commanded the man to receive his miracle. Four days later, the same doctors reported that his cancer was in remission. Praise the Lord Jesus Christ. Why was she able to pray for a dying man with such confidence? She recognized by faith that healing was her divine right. She believed with all of her heart that healing is truly "the children's bread."

SUMMARY QUESTIONS

1. How would you define healing?

2. What is meant by the term "the children's bread"?

3. Why is healing such an important reality to understand and embrace?

4. What is the difference between a right and a privilege?

HEALING PRAYER

Father, in the name of Jesus, I thank You for all that You have done. I thank You that healing is "the children's bread." From this day forward, I will see healing as a divine right rather than something I need to beg and plead to receive. I declare that I am the healed of the Lord, and through Your Holy Spirit I will take Your healing power to the nations. I embrace the reality of divine healing in my life! In Jesus's name. Amen!

CHAPTER 3

HEALING IN REDEMPTION

ealing is the manifestation of God's supernatural power and promises in the lives of believers, particularly the spiritual, emotional, and physical being. We discovered earlier that healing is the children's bread; it is a divine right. What is the basis for divine healing? What gives us the right to be healed? The redemptive work of Christ on the cross is what gives us that right. The Bible says that Jesus "bare our sins in his own body on the tree." What does this mean? To understand this concept let us look to the Old Testament. In Numbers, the Bible says this:

> *And the Lord sent fiery serpents among the people, and they bit the people; and much people of Israel died. Therefore the people came to Moses, and said, We have sinned, for we have spoken against the Lord, and against thee; pray unto the Lord, that he take away the serpents from us. And Moses prayed for the people. And the Lord said unto*

> *Moses, Make thee a fiery serpent, and set it upon a pole: and it shall come to pass, that every one that is bitten, when he looketh upon it, shall live. And Moses made a serpent of brass, and put it upon a pole, and it came to pass, that if a serpent had bitten any man, when he beheld the serpent of brass, he lived* (Numbers 21:6-9).

In this passage of Scripture, we see that the children of Israel were under God's wrath and judgment for speaking against God and Moses. The result of this judgment was fiery serpents that began biting the Israelites to the point of death. The word used for fiery serpent is the Hebrew word *saraph*, which means "poison or burning." It also means "seraph or seraphim." A seraphim was an angel or messenger. I believe that this is symbolic of the spiritual nature of this particular judgment, and sin as a whole. Once the Israelites realized their sin, they immediately repented and asked Moses to pray to God on their behalf. God told Moses to make a brass serpent and place it on a pole (see Num. 21:8). Whenever a fiery serpent bit someone, they would look upon the serpent of brass and live.

This is a very powerful type and shadow of the redemptive work of Christ. Jesus said in John 3:14-15, "And as Moses lifted up the serpent in the wilderness, even so must the Son of man be lifted up: that whosoever believeth in him should not perish, but have eternal life." Jesus became the "serpent of brass" that took away judgment from the people of God. He was lifted up on the cross, so that whoever places their faith and trust in Him would have eternal life. Notice, the Bible didn't just say that we would be saved; it said that we would have "eternal life." This is the Greek word *zoe*, which literally means the same life God has in Himself. This is a life of completeness and wholeness. Jesus took death and judgment upon Himself so that you and I could receive eternal life—which includes health, wholeness, and victory. The Israelites were instantly healed the moment they looked upon the serpent. Why? The brass serpent represented substitution—it took the place of their death and judgment in order to give them life. In the same way, Jesus became a curse for us so that we would no longer have to live under the curse.

HE BECAME A CURSE FOR US

The Bible says in Galatians 3:13, "Christ hath redeemed us from the curse of the law, being made a curse for us: for it is written, Cursed is every one that hangeth on a tree." The cross represents the curse. In fact, during the time of the Roman Empire, crucifixion was the most severe and shameful of all deaths. Jesus Christ became the curse of sin, death, poverty, and sickness so that we might receive the blessing of righteousness, eternal life, abundance, and divine health. We received the opposite of the curse as the result of Christ's sacrifice. He took upon Himself the bite of the "fiery serpent" of sin and death for us. Those of us who believe in Jesus were redeemed.

What does it mean to be redeemed? The word *redeemed* (as found in Galatians 3:13) comes from the Greek word *exagorazō*, which means "the payment of a price to recover from the power of another, to ransom, or buy off" (Strong's, G1805). Simply put, you and I have a right to divine healing through the redemptive sacrifice of Jesus Christ. The Bible says that with His stripes we were healed (see 1 Pet. 2:24). The word *stripes* comes from the Greek word *mōlōps*, which means "a wound trickling with blood" (Strong's, G3468). The stripes mentioned in First Peter are referencing the Roman punishment of scourging. This was a very horrible method of interrogating criminals. During scourging, the flesh was viciously torn from the back and legs. Every stripe upon the body of Jesus Christ brought about our healing and deliverance.

When you look at sickness from this vantage point, it dramatically changes the way you approach infirmity in your life and the lives of your loved ones. God allowing His own Son to be scourged and subsequently crucified is proof positive that He wants you and I well. The next time you think of a physical sickness, I want you to remember the price that Jesus paid. You don't have the right to be oppressed by sickness considering the depth of Christ's sacrifice for you. Did you know that the moment you became born again you stepped into an inheritance of health and healing?

YOUR BODY IS A TEMPLE!

Not only are we healed in redemption, but the moment we became born again (accepted Jesus Christ as Lord and Savior) our body became the temple of the Holy Spirit. According to First Corinthians 6:19, our bodies are the temple of God's Spirit and we were bought with a price. This means that Jesus owns every part of your being. What if every Christian began to live their lives as if they were not their own? This is what the Bible says:

For ye are bought with a price: therefore glorify God in your body, and in your spirit, which are God's (1 Corinthians 6:20).

The word *bought* (*agorazō*) means "to purchase something in the market." Jesus bought us back from the devil. Before we were saved, we were Satan's property. The moment we accepted Christ, we became God's property. As His property, He chooses what He wants to do with us. Interestingly enough, God chooses to live on the inside of us. Our body becomes His dwelling place. Not only does He make our body His dwelling, but He also refers to us as "the temple." The word *temple* comes from the Greek word *naos,* meaning "sacred edifice." God calls us His sacred tabernacle, His holy place. Imagine, then, how God feels when sickness comes into our body and desecrates the temple

When I was growing up, we were not allowed to eat food or chew gum in church, especially not in the sanctuary. Many people would end up placing gum under their seat or spilling food on the floor. How disrespectful of them! Why would they operate with such deep disregard and inconsideration in the house of God? Jesus shared a similar zeal for the house of God. The Bible records:

And Jesus went into the temple of God, and cast out all them that sold and bought in the temple, and overthrew the tables of the moneychangers, and the seats of them that sold doves, and said unto them, It is written, My house shall be called the house of prayer; but ye have made it a den of thieves (Matthew 21:12-13).

YOU ARE A HOUSE OF PRAYER

Jesus became furious when He saw the physical abuse of the temple. Why? He understood the true sanctity of the temple, and He recognized that this sanctity was being violated. The truth is that the physical church building is nothing compared to your physical body. You, not the physical church building, are His dwelling place. How much more vigilant should you be in stewarding over God's house of prayer?

This is the reason why healing is so vitally important in the world today. Divine healing enables the people of God to fulfill their divine purpose in the earth as individual "houses of prayer." Imagine a brother coming to you and saying that he was involved in sexual sin. You would probably instantly correct him and tell him to repent. Why? His body is the temple of God. This is why the Bible says that you are to "glorify God in your body, and in your spirit, which are God's" (1 Cor. 6:20). You are a courier of the glory of God.

In the same way that God doesn't want sexual sin in the temple, He is equally zealous against sickness in the temple. When was the last time you told someone that God was allowing them to commit adultery to teach them a lesson? That seems pretty ridiculous, doesn't it? Why? Adultery defiles a person from the inside out—this is explicitly stated in First Corinthians 6:18. God would never desecrate His own temple to prove a point. Why then do people believe that God desires that their bodies be desecrated with sickness and disease, especially to prove a point?

Now, I want to take a moment and clarify something. I am in no way suggesting that if you are sick you are somehow "dirty" or "defiled"; I am saying that you should be as zealous concerning sickness as you are concerning sin. Stop tolerating sickness in your life! It is not from God! Too many in the church have taken a passive stance when it comes to the temple of the Holy Ghost. Now is the time for us to rise up in zeal and passion and drive out sickness and disease. It is time for us to tell the devil, "My body is the temple of the Holy Spirit, I am a house of prayer, and therefore I give you no place!"

THE POWER OF PASSOVER

And thus shall ye eat it; with your loins girded, your shoes on your feet, and your staff in your hand; and ye shall eat it in haste: it is the Lord's Passover. For I will pass through the land of Egypt this night, and will smite all the firstborn in the land of Egypt, both man and beast; and against all the gods of Egypt I will execute judgment: I am the Lord (Exodus 12:11-12).

God is and has always been jealous over His children, even from the very beginning. We can see this truth expressed throughout the Old Testament. Time and time again, we see the Lord fighting for Israel. In the book of Exodus, God delivered the Israelites out of captivity after 430 years of Egyptian bondage. He raised up Moses as a prophet and deliverer to His people (which is a prophetic foreshadowing of Jesus Christ the Messiah). Through a series of plagues, God released judgment upon Egypt and its pharaoh for refusing to let God's people go. The last plague (which is the one we will concentrate on the most) has profound spiritual significance for us today, especially as it relates to divine healing. In Exodus, we see that God issued one last plague:

> *And all the firstborn in the land of Egypt shall die, from the firstborn of Pharaoh that sitteth upon his throne, even unto the firstborn of the maidservant that is behind the mill; and all the firstborn of beasts* (Exodus 11:5).

God told Moses that this plague would cause Pharaoh to let the Israelites go. You must understand that the firstborn was very significant. The firstborn was heir to the kingdom; therefore, by killing the firstborn, God was in essence cutting off the inheritance of Egypt. However, God made provision for His people—the Passover. The Israelites were to take a lamb and roast it and place the blood of that lamb on the doorpost (see Exod. 12:13). By doing this, the spirit of death would pass over them. In other words, they were exonerated from judgment through the covenant of Passover. This is amazing! God also told them to eat the

Passover with unleavened bread (yeast or leaven was symbolic of the sin of Egypt). They were to eat the Passover in haste and flee from Egypt immediately the next morning. This was the first day of the month for Israel and a new year for them as a nation. God was establishing an ordinance that the Israelites were to observe forever.

What is the significance of this Passover and what does it have to do with healing? I am glad you asked! The Passover represents the atoning sacrifice of Jesus Christ as our Passover Lamb who caused death to pass over us forever. Passover also represents the establishment of a new system, separate from that of Egypt. God was setting Israel apart as a holy nation to Himself. This was amazing in and of itself, but God didn't stop there. Through the Passover, the Israelites received divine healing and supernatural restoration. The Bible says, "He brought them forth also with silver and gold: and there was not one feeble person among their tribes" (Ps. 105:37). The word for "feeble" is the Hebrew word *kashal* (Strong's, H3782), "to totter, stumble, or stagger." It is the walk of those who are physically sick or weak from dehydration, disease, or other physical infirmity.

It would be reasonable to assume that after 430 years of slavery almost all the Israelites would be tottering. Why were none of them weak? The key was the Passover. I believe that the Passover feast, as a prophetic act, released the supernatural power of God into their physical bodies. They were miraculously healed in an instant. Hallelujah! If the Israelites were supernaturally healed and restored by observing Passover, how much more are you and I healed and restored in Christ, our Passover Lamb? They were healed under the shadow; we are healed under the substance! The next time you are wondering whether or not it is God's will for you to be healed, remember the Passover—Jesus Christ.

HEALING TESTIMONY

Communion is something that we regularly observe in our church. In fact, we take it every Sunday. One particular Sunday, I was teaching on the communion and its connection to Christ's atoning sacrifice for us and the blessing of healing as a result of that sacrifice. After communion, a lady expressed that someone close to her had been suspected of having testicular cancer. The doctors set up another visit to do a further biopsy. We declared that the blood of Jesus paid the penalty for that cancer, and we released the healing power of God over this person. A few days later, the doctors reported that there was nothing on his testicles. The cancer had completely vanished. Hallelujah!

SUMMARY QUESTIONS

1. What is the relationship between healing and redemption?

2. How did Jesus become a curse for us?

3. What does the Bible mean when it says, "Your body is the temple of the Holy Ghost"?

4. What does the term house of prayer mean? How does it apply to you?

5. What was the power and result of the Passover?

CHAPTER 4

THE POWER TO HEAL

And he ordained twelve, that they should be with him, and that he might send them forth to preach, and to have power to heal sicknesses, and to cast out devils (Mark 3:14-15).

There is a very disturbing myth in the church today (we will deal with healing myths in more detail in a later chapter) which suggests that healing is no longer relevant for the times in which we live. Not only does Scripture not support this, but also it is downright ridiculous. Healing is more relevant now than it has ever been before. However, there is something even more insidious and malevolent at work in the church today; that is the notion that healing is reserved for a particular healing minister, television personality, or "special person." As a result of this wrong philosophy, people are ignorant of the power that Jesus gave *all* of us to heal the sick. That's right! You have been given supernatural power by God to heal the sick.

In the Gospel of Mark, Jesus equipped His disciples with the power to heal. The Bible records: "That He might send them forth to preach, and to have power to heal sicknesses, and to cast out devils" (Mark 3:14-15). Why did Jesus give them power to heal the sick? First of all, we must define what is meant by the term *power*. The word *power* written in this passage is the Greek word *exousia* (Strong's, G1849), "the right or authority to act" or "physical and mental power." In other words, Jesus gave them the authority to heal the sick. This authority was not just manifested in spiritual terms, but in pragmatic terms as well. They were endued with the divine right and ability to heal the sick spiritually, physically, and emotionally.

By *heal* we are referring to the service of curing or restoring people to health. Notice that this power was given the moment they were commissioned by Christ to preach the gospel. Why? If you preach a gospel that says that Jesus is Lord and the Kingdom of God is supreme, it must include the manifestation of supernatural power. Why would someone believe in a God who is powerless against sickness and disease?

For years the church has neglected one of the most fundamental aspects of preaching the gospel—healing. What if I told you that you have just as much authority to heal the sick as the apostles of the first century church? Well, guess what? You do! The point is that they were given power to heal the sick in order to confirm the gospel of the Kingdom of God. They were also given power to heal the sick in order to release people from satanic oppression. After all, the gospel is the "good news." Jesus came to set the captives free according to Luke 4:18.

THE GREAT OMISSION

When I was coming up in church, we were taught to believe that Jesus was the Healer. I was raised in a Spirit-filled church, so everyone I knew embraced the gifts of the Spirit, at least in theory. The problem was, I did not regularly see church members healing the sick. In fact, I can't recall a single time where a group of young people in the church went out to pray for the sick. Now that I think about it, this is very disturbing. To be honest, I saw more sickness than I saw people healing the sick. I often refer to this as cognitive dissonance. This is when a belief that a person holds is inconsistent with their behavior. So, we were saying that Jesus was the Healer, but we weren't walking in this reality.

Many people have experienced this problem. In fact, there are entire denominations built on the gifts of the Spirit, yet if you were to attend their services you would see little if any gifts operating at all. We have somehow replaced "The Great Commission" with "The Great Omission." We have subconsciously omitted the power of the resurrection from Christianity. I remember sitting in church as a young person scratching my head. Why were so many Christians being ravaged by sickness and disease? Why weren't we doing anything about it?

There are many reasons, but the main one, I believe, is the fact that we have embraced a passive form of spirituality. It seems we have been taught (either through explicit teaching or lack thereof) to be spiritual spectators. Even our churches have been designed architecturally to mimic theaters or auditoriums, thus encouraging an "entertainment" or "spectator" culture. It is almost like we are attending a movie or theatrical play. People are encouraged to come to a "comfortable" atmosphere and "receive"—maybe even have a cup of coffee while they're at it. I am not against innovation or megachurches or being progressive in our approach to ministry, but I am concerned that we have departed from the New Testament model of active and engaged Christianity. The Christian life is to be filled with consistent displays of God's supernatural power—especially healing.

The reality is that we live in a fallen world that desperately needs Jesus and all that He has to offer. How do we accomplish this mandate? The first thing that we need to do is recognize what we have been given in Christ. We must realize that it is the will of God to heal the sick and to restore the broken. Once we realize that this is God's plan, the next thing that we need to do is come to the realization that He wants to use us to do it. You may be saying, "I am not ready or prepared!" The disciples were not prepared either. In fact, they were a band of misfits who barely understood anything that Jesus had to say, yet He still used them. God is no respecter of persons. If He can use publicans, tax collectors, and uneducated fisherman, then surely He can use you!

WHAT ARE YOU WAITING FOR?

Several years ago, my wife and I were attending a John G. Lake seminar in Florida. The minister came from out of town to teach on divine healing. Scores of people lined up to receive their healing. There were all kinds of infirmities represented in the room, including arthritis, gout, cancer, diabetes, mental retardation, lupus, heart disease, and many more. I must admit that, though I wasn't sick, I too was looking forward to seeing some sort of miraculous display. You can imagine my surprise when the minister stood up in front of the room and said that he wasn't going to heal anybody. This was not what I expected at all! He looked around the room and asked people to raise their hand if they were sick. After many people raised their hands, he paused for a moment and said, "Well, what are you waiting for? Go pray for the sick!"

I was shocked by the audacity of his statement. Did he expect us to actually go and heal our brothers and sisters? Apparently he did! The interesting thing about all of this was that people began to run around the room praying for the sick. They were actually doing as they were instructed. As I began to join others in praying for the sick, an amazing thing happened—the power of God began to manifest. People started to grab me asking me to pray for them. I don't have medical reports to prove it, but I know beyond the shadow of a doubt that many were healed. I also know that something inside me changed. I realized that God was waiting on us to do what He has empowered us to do.

What are you waiting for today? Are you waiting for a title or an ordination certificate? Those things have no relevance to the power already resident in you. Furthermore, God has already ordained you. You were ordained the moment you became born again to do as Jesus did. I know it may seem a bit strange, but God is waiting for you! I can imagine the reaction of the disciples when Jesus told them to go. They were probably terrified by the thought of facing the leprous, blind, crippled, were demon possessed. Talk about on-the-job training! Yet Jesus knew that their success was not predicated on them, but on Him. The Bible says:

> *And these signs shall follow them that believe; In my name shall they cast out devils; they shall speak with new tongues; they shall take up serpents; and if they drink any deadly thing, it shall not hurt them; they shall lay hands on the sick, and they shall recover* (Mark 16:17-18).

Notice that the Bible says, "These signs shall follow them that believe," which means that the only requirement to heal the sick is faith and confidence in Jesus Christ. The burden to manifest healing is on Him. Why? Because He was the one who told us to go! The Bible says that we shall lay hands on the sick and they shall recover. The phrase "shall recover" is the combination of two Greek words—*echō* and *kalōs*. These words are written in the imperative and when used together mean "to hold or possess excellent and complete restoration to health" (Strong's, G2192, G2573). It's a guarantee—those whom we pray for will be restored to health. Period!

This is a promise that we are to possess by faith. Notice that this recovery has nothing to do with the acclaim or ability of the person ministering the healing. It has everything to do with God who promised that these "signs" or "marks" would follow those of us who believe. The word *signs* (*semeion* in Greek) means miracles and wonders by which God authenticates the men sent by Him, or by which men prove that the cause they are pleading is God's. Have you considered that you have been called to plead God's cause in the earth? This is what it means to preach or proclaim the gospel. We are declaring the message of God's Kingdom throughout the earth, and God has given the gift of healing to His church in order to authenticate this message.

COMMISSIONED WITH POWER

And Jesus came and spake unto them, saying, All power is given unto me in heaven and in earth. Go ye therefore, and teach all nations, baptizing them in the name of the Father, and of the Son, and of the Holy Ghost: teaching them to observe all things whatsoever I have commanded you: and, lo, I am with you always, even unto the end of the world. Amen (Matthew 28:18-20).

In the Gospel of Matthew, Jesus commissioned His disciples (not just the twelve) to go into all the world and teach all nations, baptizing them in the name of the Father, and of the Son, and of the Holy Ghost. Notice that in the previous verse, Jesus declares: "All power is given unto me in heaven and in earth." What does this mean? It means that Jesus Christ has inherited *all* power from the Father. Not only did He inherit *all* power from the Father, but He has the authority to execute that power in both heaven and earth. Many people believe that Jesus has authority in heaven, but they fail to acknowledge His authority in the earth. That's saying He can save your soul but not heal your body; this is unscriptural. The word *all* suggests that every power or authority that exists is subject to His power and authority. There is nothing more powerful than Jesus Christ, including sickness and disease.

With that said, it is important to understand the way a kingdom operates. In ancient kingdoms, a king was the person who possessed the authority in the land. He was literally the law. He determined who lived and who died, who paid taxes and who didn't. Whenever a king delegated authority to someone, that person was vested with the same authority that the king himself possessed. When Jesus Christ rose from the grave, He possessed all the power resident within the Kingdom of God; by telling us to "go," we were endued with that same power. He delegated His authority to us! We are His vice regents in the earth. Jesus used the Greek word *poreuō*, which means "to transfer" (Strong's, G4198). The moment Jesus said "go," you and I were commissioned with supernatural power and authority to carry out His mandate in heaven and in earth. The authority is the legal right to operate in a particular domain and the power is the ability to carry out that authority. Where is our jurisdiction? Heaven and earth! When it comes to sickness, we have the right and the ability to make sickness bow to us, just like it bowed before Jesus Himself.

What does this authority look like? For one, it means that you and I no longer need to be intimidated by sickness anymore. It means that there is no such thing as big sicknesses and small sicknesses anymore; any and all sickness must bow to the power we possess. You must realize that this power was part of a package deal. It is part and parcel with the new birth. (We realize that we must be filled with the Spirit of God as well.) Remember, this is not a commission from man but of Christ Himself, the Supreme Ruler of the universe. Take a few moments and process what I just said! What are you waiting for? Go and heal the sick today!

HEALING PRAYER

Father, in the name of Jesus Christ, I thank You that You have empowered me to heal the sick. Thank You, Lord, that we are no longer subjected to sickness and disease, but sickness and disease are subjected to us. I stand in bold confidence knowing that my ability to heal the sick is not based on my ability at all, but on Your power and Great Commission. Thank You for commissioning me to preach the gospel of the Kingdom of God and to penetrate the kingdom of darkness for Your glory. Use me to heal the sick, to raise the dead, and to deliver the captives from this day forward. I lay aside all fear and insecurity and I go! In Jesus's name, amen!

SUMMARY QUESTIONS

1. What is the power to heal?

2. Why has the church at large neglected their commission to heal the sick?

3. What did Jesus tell His disciples before His ascension (according to Matthew 28:18-20)?

4. Why do we believe that something has to "happen" before we can pray for the sick?

CHAPTER 5

CHRIST'S AUTHORITY IN US

And as ye go, preach, saying, The kingdom of heaven is at hand. Heal the sick, cleanse the lepers, raise the dead, cast out devils: freely ye have received, freely give (Matthew 10:7-8).

Earlier, we mentioned the profound implications of delegated authority. We discovered that Christ has in fact delegated authority to His body, the Church. By *authority* we mean the lawful right to execute the plan and purposes of God in the earth, including healing the sick, raising the dead, and casting out demons. Just as military generals are given military authority to war on behalf of a kingdom, so you and I have been given the right to wage war on the powers of darkness. However, you and I have not simply received delegated authority. Our authority goes even deeper—we possess Christ's authority inside of us by the Spirit. This authority is encapsulated within the resurrected Christ resident inside us as believers. This means that it is more than just following the orders and commands of an external King, but it means that the King of kings is actually manifesting His power and authority in and through us. In John 15, the Bible says:

> *I am the vine, ye are the branches: He that abideth in me, and I in him, the same bringeth forth much fruit: for without me ye can do nothing* (John 15:5).

The word *abide* in this passage of Scripture means "to remain" or "sojourn." The word picture is that of a traveler taking rest in a particular residence. In this case, we are to rest in His authority. Just like a branch is inextricably connected to the vine, so are we connected to Christ by virtue of the new birth. Through this connection, you and I are able to manifest fruit that remains. In other words, we are able to display the power and authority of Christ Himself. This is why the Bible says, "Without me ye can do nothing" (John 15:5). When you really internalize this powerful truth, you will realize that it is not you doing anything, but His authority working through you.

No More Intimidation

My wife and I teach and train people to walk in divine healing through various healing schools and supernatural schools of ministry. One night at our healing school, a young man brought a friend of his down to the altar who had been viciously attacked. Her ex-boyfriend kicked this young lady in the eye; her eyeball had exploded in the socket. The doctors said that she would never see out of that eye again nor would there be any activity. In fact, they were preparing to give her a glass eye.

The moment I saw her condition, I became very intimidated. I was looking at things from the natural perspective. As we prayed for her, there was no outward manifestation of healing. We asked if she had forgiven everyone, if she desired to be healed, and so on. Even though I had seen God perform very extravagant healings in the past, something about her scenario gave me pause. As we prayed for her, the tear ducts began to loosen and she started to cry out of the dead eye. However, we did not see the full manifestation of her healing that night. Later that night during my devotion time, I asked God why the young lady didn't get healed completely. Was it her lack of faith? God said to me, "It was not her lack of faith; it was yours!" I realized in that moment that I had allowed myself to become intimidated by her condition. Why? I was relying on my own ability instead of abiding in the authority of Christ.

Fear neutralizes faith and hinders the manifestation of healing and miracles.

From that day on, I decided that I would never be afraid or intimidated by any form of sickness, disease, or ailment again. At the next healing school, a young lady came down who had a stroke recently and lost the use of her right arm and her vocal cords. She could not say a single intelligible word. I decided that I was going to give the devil a black eye that night. I asked her to tell me what was wrong with her; she laughed while her friend gently explained to me, "She can't speak!"

I asked her again, "What is going on with you?" She struggled to get out a single word. I commanded the vocal cords to be loosed and the nervous system to be restored in the name of Jesus.

All of a sudden, the lady screamed, "Hallelujah!" As I continued to tell her to repeat after me she said, "J-j-j-eee-sus, Jee-sus, Jesus!" The entire congregation exploded with praise and thanksgiving. The more she shouted, the more faith arose in the atmosphere.

Afterward, I asked her to use her hand; her friend explained, "She can't use her hand!"

I told her to take the microphone out of my hand, and she grabbed it and shouted "Hallelujah!"

Praise the Lord! In a matter of minutes, God healed her vocal chords and restored the use of her arm. This is what happens when you and I no longer look to our own ability and righteousness, but instead choose to step into the very authority of Christ in us. Unlike the previous scenario, I endeavored to see the condition the way Jesus saw it. He has all authority and there is no sickness or disease that can stand before Him; therefore, there is no sickness that can stand before me. Refuse to be intimidated!

WE ARE SONS AND DAUGHTERS

But as many as received him, to them gave he power to become the sons of God, even to them that believe on his name (John 1:12).

It is extremely important for us to know our identity if we are going to successfully flow in the power of God, particularly healing the sick. We must understand that we are not simply followers of Jesus, but we are children of God. The Bible says those of us who have received Him have been given the right or authority to become sons of God (see John 1:12). The word *received* is a very important word. It comes from the Greek word *lambano*, "to take with the hand." It means to grab hold of something with a sense of entitlement.

We must embrace our sonship. Why? It belongs to us! Jesus paid a tremendous price to make you and me sons and daughters of God. Only those who accept and receive their sonship by faith will walk in their true identity. It is important to note that the concept of spiritual sonship is gender neutral. Both male and female are sons of God in Christ Jesus, in an ontological sense. When we come into the consciousness of our sonship, it will cause us to experience a supernatural mega thrust in our spiritual lives. With sonship comes spiritual authority. Jesus never negotiated with demons or rationalized sickness. Instead, He saw sickness and disease as enemies of the Kingdom of God and dealt with them accordingly. He was able to function this way because He was absolutely secure in His relationship with God the Father. What an amazing God we serve! He so longed to save and deliver us that He wrapped Himself in frail humanity just to redeem us. The amazing thing is that you and I are incarnated with the same risen Christ who overcame sin, sickness, death, and hell.

> *We possess the DNA of the Father inside our very being and therefore carry the same authority to heal the sick that Christ possessed on the earth.*

Can you imagine this? You are not simply using a bunch of complex formulas to conjure supernatural manifestations, but you are a son or daughter of God releasing His divine power in the earth. You are inextricably connected to the Vine (Jesus), and through this connection you are empowered to operate in His authority.

I want you to take a moment and think about what it means to be a child of God. When I was younger, I can remember my father picking me up from school. I was always excited to see him. I enjoyed spending time with him. Ultimately, I wanted to be my father. To me, he represented strength, authority, masculinity, and power. Everywhere I went, people who knew my father would automatically know that I was his son. This is what it means to be a child of God. All that He embodies is manifested in us. We should look, think, act, and speak like our Father. When people see us they should see Him and vice versa. What will your spiritual and physical life look like once you realize that God is truly your Father? From this day forward you no longer need to fear or be intimidated by the power of the devil. We are children of the Most High God!

AUTHORITY OVER THE ENEMY

Behold, I give unto you power to tread on serpents and scorpions, and over all the power of the enemy: and nothing shall by any means hurt you (Luke 10:19).

Now that you realize that God has given you authority, you need to know how this authority works. In Luke 10:19, Jesus gave the disciples authority to tread on serpents and scorpions and over all the power of the enemy. What does this mean? Well, it means that you and I have been given the authority to dominate over all demonic forces. I love the way this is articulated in the Greek: "Behold, I bestow the gift of power of rule and government to trample under foot serpents and poisonous scorpions and over all the strength, power, and ability of the hideous, hated, and hostile one, and nothing shall cause you damage or harm" (my adaptation from Greek definitions). Notice that we have authority but the devil has power. What is the difference? Authority is the legal right to act on behalf of someone else—in this case Jesus Christ.

This means that all of heaven will enforce what we do or say according to the Word of God. Satan, on the other hand, is a fallen rogue angel, who has been rejected by God and the

Kingdom of heaven at large. He has no support system for what he does, other than his demons. He has no authority! In this sense, you and I are much more powerful than the devil. Why is this so important? Acts 10:38 says, "How God anointed Jesus of Nazareth with the Holy Ghost and with power: who went about doing good, and healing all that were oppressed of the devil; for God was with him." Jesus went about healing, curing, and releasing those who were under the devil's oppression. What did this oppression look like? Sickness and disease! We also have been given authority by God to tread over Satan's power by healing the sick. This is exactly what Jesus did. Later we will talk about the relationship between healing and deliverance, but for now I want you to understand that sickness is essentially the oppression of the devil. By healing the sick we are expanding God's Kingdom agenda in the earth. We are revealing His heart of goodness to the world. We are setting the captives free!

> *Jesus has given us the rule of government to dominate over sickness, disease, and infirmity. The shed blood of Jesus Christ ratified this authority.*

IT'S EASIER THAN YOU THINK!

During one of our services, we were teaching on spiritual authority. After I taught for a while, I decided that people needed to see what we were talking about. I told them to stand up if they were facing any physical challenges or symptoms in their bodies. Several people stood up. One young man had been suffering from severe back pain and leg pain. As he stood, I called another young lady, who happened to be very new in her walk with Christ. I told her to place her hand on his back and command the pain to leave in Jesus's name. She asked if that was all she had to do. "Yep, that's all!" I exclaimed.

So she said, "In the name of Jesus Christ, I command this back pain to leave now!"

I asked the young man if he felt any pain, and he said, "No! Not at all!" The young lady was amazed by how easy it seemed to be.

You may be thinking, "It can't be that easy!" You're right, if you are relying on yourself. However, if you are relying on Him, that is another story. You must realize that Christ already conquered sickness. He already did the hard work. Furthermore, He has given us His authority to dominate over the power of the enemy. Once you realize that you have authority and that sickness is from the devil, you can easily address it.

You may be saying, "Well that was only back pain!" Remember, there are no degrees of sickness from God's perspective. He is eternal and all powerful. He doesn't exert any more energy on cancer than He does on a common cold. To prove my point even further, I will share with you another healing testimony.

HEALING TESTIMONY

We were holding a healing meeting one night. During this meeting, I taught on the power of expectation. The Lord told me to build expectation in the people so that they could receive the manifestation of their healing. I talked about the widow woman of Zarephath in First Kings 17. I said that the containers of oil represented expectation.

As I was teaching, the Holy Spirit gave me a word of knowledge about a young woman who had been physically abused by her significant other and was dealing with anxiety. I asked this person to come forward and no one moved at all. I knew that I had heard from God so I continued to insist. Thank God I did, because the moment I was about to move on, a young lady came down to the altar with a shameful face and tears in her eyes. She said that she did not want to come forward because she was too embarrassed. Then she revealed that she had three lumps on her breast. All of the things she underwent had caused a tremendous amount of anxiety inside her mind and physical body. Before I laid hands on her, I felt impressed to speak the Word of God over her. I told her that she would not die, but live and declare the works of the Lord according to Psalm 118:17. I cursed the cancer and spoke life over her body. She immediately fell to the ground weeping.

Afterward, she approached me and told me that when she checked her breast, every lump had disappeared. Hallelujah to the Lamb of God. I didn't sweat, jump, moan, or growl to manifest her healing. I didn't say a series of prepackaged prayers; all I did was agree with God that it was His will for her to be healed. I simply released my faith and rested in the authority of Jesus. It is just that easy! You may have a loved one or member of your church who needs healing; don't wait for someone else to pray. You have the authority in you to heal the sick. Place a demand on it by faith!

WE ARE AMBASSADORS OF CHRIST

Now then we are ambassadors for Christ, as though God did beseech you by us: we pray you in Christ's stead, be ye reconciled to God (2 Corinthians 5:20).

In John 20:21, the Bible says, "Then said Jesus to them again, Peace be unto you: as my Father hath sent me, even so send I you." This is one of the most powerful statements in the Bible. In this we see that after His resurrection, Jesus sent His disciples to accomplish a specific assignment on His behalf—to preach the gospel of the Kingdom. Just as the Father sent Jesus to fulfill His assignment, so Christ has sent us to fulfill His Kingdom mandate. What does it mean to be sent? The word *sent* comes from the Greek word *apostellō* and means "to be sent with orders." This is the verb form to the Greek noun *apostolos*, which means "one who is sent" or "delegate." This concept comes from an ancient Roman and Phoenician governmental title. In those days, an "apostle" was a person sent out by the king with specific instructions or orders.

> *Jesus has sent us and given us ambassadorial
> authority to represent Him in the earth.*

This instruction included the apostolic power and authority to carry out the assignment for which they were sent. Jesus is the Apostle and High Priest of our profession (see Heb. 3:1). He was sent by God the Father on a redemptive assignment to deliver you and me from the power of darkness. As the Apostle of our faith, He has sent us and endued us with the same authority that He possesses. In other words, we are His ambassadors. An ambassador is an accredited diplomat sent by a country as its official representative to a foreign land. We are Christ's ambassadors in the earth. With ambassadorship comes the authority to represent Jesus in word and action. Whatever God intends in the earth, He has given us the legislative authority to facilitate. God intends for people to be healed and delivered; therefore, He has empowered us to heal the sick. When we command the sick to be healed, He is commanding the sick to be healed. There is no difference in authority! We are carriers of His power and authority, and when we speak all the powers of darkness must take heed. So instead of cowering before sickness, tell that disease where to sit; all of heaven will support you! This understanding will transform your life.

HEALING PRAYER

Father, in the name of Jesus Christ I thank You that I am an ambassador of Jesus. Through You I have been given the power and authority to carry out Your redemptive plan in the earth. Right now, in Jesus's name, I take authority over every sickness, disease, and infirmity, and I command them to leave me now. I declare that I will lay hands on the sick and they shall recover. I recognize today that the authority that I carry within is the same as Jesus Christ Himself. Today, I confidently apply Your Word and I walk in the faith and boldness to heal the sick. In Jesus's name. Amen!

SUMMARY QUESTIONS

1. What type of authority has Christ given us?

2. What does this authority imply?

3. What are the spiritual and physical implications of sonship?

4. What does it mean to be an ambassador of Christ?

CHAPTER 6

THREE DIMENSIONS
OF HEALING

The Spirit of the Lord is upon me, because he hath anointed me to preach the gospel to the poor; he hath sent me to heal the brokenhearted, to preach deliverance to the captives, and recovering of sight to the blind, to set at liberty them that are bruised, to preach the acceptable year of the Lord (Luke 4:18-19).

When Adam and Eve fell in the Garden of Eden, they fell totally. This means that they were affected by their fall from God's grace in every area of their lives. In fact, Adam and Eve underwent three dimensions of death (which we will address in a moment). If the redemptive purpose of God was to be effective, it had to address all three areas.

Jesus's earthly ministry addressed the tripartite nature of man in its entirety and the need to experience total healing and deliverance, thus reflecting God's redemptive will in relation to humankind. In Luke 4:18-19, the Bible says that the Spirit of the Lord was upon Jesus and anointed Him to minister in the following categories: preaching the gospel to the poor, healing the brokenhearted, preaching deliverance to the captives and recovery of sight to the blind, setting at liberty them that are bruised, proclaiming the acceptable year of the Lord. God had to manifest His healing power in all three of the areas in which man fell. In the same manner, if you and I are going to minister healing and reconciliation, we must confront these areas as well. There are three significant dimensions to healing.

1. SPIRITUAL HEALING

The first area of healing that Jesus addressed was spiritual healing. What is meant by the term *spiritual healing*? Well, if man is essentially a spiritual being, then the foundation of his sickness is spiritual in nature. In the book of Isaiah, the Bible says, "But he was wounded for our transgressions, he was bruised for our iniquities: the chastisement of our peace was upon him; and with his stripes we are healed" (Isa. 53:5). Notice that the text says, "He was wounded for our transgressions." The Hebrew word for *transgression* means "guilt of transgression." Christ was literally the guilt offering for our transgressions against God.

This guilt (resulting from sin) alienates people from God and keeps them bound to sin. Therefore, spiritual healing is the restoration of our spiritual connection to God. This connection was severed by sin, and Jesus came to restore that connection through His atoning (and remitting) sacrifice on the cross. Remember, sickness was introduced to the world through sin (transgression), and as a result the human race fell into "spiritual sickness" or "sin sickness." So the first dimension of healing is the reconciliation of our spiritual man. It is also important to note that through sin, the human race was opened to spiritual oppression. Jesus came to "set at liberty those who were oppressed." Spiritual oppression is at the core of many illnesses and diseases. To illustrate spiritual healing further, we can take a look at the woman with the infirmity found in Luke's account:

> *And, behold, there was a woman which had a spirit of infirmity eighteen years, and was bowed together, and could in no wise lift up herself. And when Jesus saw her, he called her to him, and said unto her, Woman, thou art loosed from thine infirmity* (Luke 13:11-12).

Jesus discerned by the Holy Spirit that her infirmity was spiritual in nature. In fact, the reason why she was bowed over (contorted) was because she was under satanic oppression (literally, "a spirit of infirmity"). Instead of laying hands on her and commanding her back to be straightened, Jesus simply said, "Woman, thou art loosed." He released her from spiritual bondage. Jesus came to bring healing to every area of our lives, especially our spiritual man. We must understand that spiritual healing is a foundational component of ministering healing to God's people.

2. HEALING OF THE SOUL

The second dimension of healing is the restoration of our soul. Isaiah 53:5 says, "The chastisement of our peace was upon Him." The word *peace* comes from the Hebrew word *shalowm*, which means "completeness, soundness, and wholeness." This is referring to the soul of man. What is the soul? The soul is the conglomerate of our mind, will, and emotions. In Luke 4, the Bible says that Jesus was sent to bind up the brokenhearted—those with shattered strength or with broken soul or mind. We see then that Jesus was not just concerned with our spiritual condition, but He is also deeply concerned with the state of our soul (i.e. mind, will, and emotions).

In the Gospel of Mark, the Bible records that there was a man possessed with devils. This man encountered Jesus and was delivered from a legion of demons inside him. In Mark 5:15, the Bible says:

> And they come to Jesus, and see him that was possessed with the devil, and had the legion, sitting, and clothed, and in his right mind: and they were afraid.

Notice that the Bible says "in his right mind." What does that term mean? The word for *right mind* is the Greek word *sōphroneō*, which means to be sound of mind. It means that God has a blueprint for the soul, and He wants our souls to function the way He intends. This is *healing of the soul*. Jesus restored the soul of that demonized man.

Hallelujah! The Bible says in Psalm 23:3, "He restoreth my soul." In essence, Jesus was fulfilling messianic prophecy by revealing Himself to the demoniac as the restorer of his soul. The beauty is that He is the same yesterday, today, and forever (see Heb. 13:8).

Whenever a person experiences restoration in their soul, that person has just undergone "soul healing." In fact, the Bible says in Acts 1:8, "But ye shall receive power, after that the Holy Ghost is come upon you: and ye shall be witnesses unto me both in Jerusalem, and in all Judaea, and in Samaria, and unto the uttermost part of the earth." Many people are familiar with this passage of Scripture, but there is much more to this verse than meets the eye. The word *power* in this passage is the Greek word *dynamis*, which among other things means moral power and excellence of soul. Wow! God wants you and me to possess "excellence of soul." This takes place when the mind, will, and emotions line up with the Word of God. We are called to minister to the soulish man just as much as we are called to minister to the physical man.

> *Jesus came to bring you and me to a place of "excellence of soul"!*

There are many denominations that teach people that Jesus only came to address humanity's spiritual condition, but this could not be further from the truth. There are so many people who are not experiencing "excellence of soul" because they are bound with bitterness, resentment, and unforgiveness. They are literally sick in their souls! The good news is that the healing power of Christ extends into the soulish realm. This includes healing from mental illness, emotional trauma, and oppression in the will.

3. PHYSICAL HEALING

Much of what you will encounter in this book addresses the physical sickness and oppression affecting God's people. Fortunately, physical healing is the most tangible of all three dimensions of healing, and as such it is what many people seek the most. There are some denominations that teach that Jesus only came to address the spiritual and emotional condition of humankind, and as such there is no precedent or basis for divine healing. Nothing could be further from the truth. Jesus came to address the spiritual, the soulish, and the physical realms. I thank God that He didn't die to only forgive my sins and heal my emotions; He also came to address the physical captivity that many face. In Luke 4, the Bible says that Jesus also came "to set at liberty them that are bruised" (Luke 4:18). The word *bruised* means "broken"—people are broken because of sickness and disease afflicting their physical bodies.

Jesus spent a significant amount of time addressing the physical sicknesses of God's people. Why? The first reason was to validate His earthly ministry. Remember, healing miracles are an expression of God's supernatural power. We mentioned earlier that healing is a means to authenticate the gospel message. The second reason is the fact that Jesus came to seek and save that which was lost (see Luke 19:10). In the Greek, the word *that* is typically expressed in the neuter, which means that Jesus was not referring to a person or people group but to a particular thing. Jesus did not simply come to save or deliver a lost people from their sin (though this is a major portion of God's redemptive plan), but in effect He came to restore "that" which was lost. What was lost? Dominion, wholeness, fellowship, and authority were lost. Acts 10:38 says:

> *How God anointed Jesus of Nazareth with the Holy Ghost and with power: who went about doing good, and healing all that were oppressed of the devil; for God was with him.*

This oppression manifested in the form of physical sickness and disease. In fact, the word *oppressed* means "to exercise harsh control over one, to use one's power against one." The devil was exercising control over the human race through sin, sickness, and disease. Think about it for a moment. Have you ever been sick? What do you think about during times of sickness? Sickness! This is the whole point— to bring you into bondage in every area of your life. Jesus released people from this bondage so that they would be in a position to hear the gospel clearly and respond accordingly. Ultimately, Jesus came to set the captives free so that they would be in a position to worship God in spirit and in truth (see John 4:23).

Lastly, physical healing is an expression of God's love for us and His desire to see us function the way He created us. We were fearfully and wonderfully made (see Ps. 139:14). God wants us to enjoy our physical lives here in the earth. He doesn't want us to be confined to a hospital bed all the days of our lives; He wants us to enjoy the earth in the way He originally intended. Adam walked with God in the cool of the day. Adam was healthy and whole all the days of His life (even after the fall). Therefore, we must understand that it is God's unconditional will to see the physically sick healed and restored in Jesus's name.

God wants us whole—spirit, soul, and body. The power of the blood of Jesus extends to the total person, not just a portion of our being. The more you realize that it is God's will for you to be whole in your total person, the more you will fight for that wholeness with all of your might. My prayer is that through the pages of this book, you will find vital keys to help empower you in becoming an effective healing minister to your friends, family, and loved ones.

HEALING PRAYER

Father, in the name of Jesus, I praise You for Your healing power working in me right now. I thank You that it is Your will to heal every aspect of my being—spirit, soul, and body. I declare that there is no weapon fashioned against me that can prosper. Your Word declares that You were my sin offering according to Isaiah 53; therefore, I receive the forgiveness of my sins through the shed blood of Jesus. First Peter 2:24 says that by Your stripes I was healed; therefore, I am the healed of the Lord from the crown of my head to the soles of my feet. The Bible says in Psalm 23 that you restore my soul; therefore, I receive the healing and restoration of my mind, will, and emotions right now in Jesus's name. Amen!

SUMMARY QUESTIONS

1. What are the three dimensions of healing?

2. Why was it important to address more than just sin?

3. What is meant by the term *guilt offering?*

4. What is the relationship between physical healing and the gospel?

CHAPTER 7

GIFT VERSUS RESPONSIBILITY

To another faith by the same Spirit; to another the gifts
of healing by the same Spirit; to another the working
of miracles; to another prophecy; to another discerning
of spirits; to another divers kinds of tongues; to another
the interpretation of tongues (1 Corinthians 12:9-10).

There is a very common misunderstanding in the church today; it is the belief that the only people who are able to heal the sick are those who possess the "gift" of healing. This assertion suggests that only a select few people who are anointed to heal the sick can get results. Consequently, there are many people who gravitate toward certain personalities or healing ministries to receive their healing miracle. I believe that there are people who operate in certain manifestations of healing and miracles based on the dispensation of God's grace by the Holy Spirit (as He wills). However, there needs to be some clarity provided on the difference between the gift (or manifestation) of healing and the responsibility that God has given every believer to heal the sick.

As I mentioned previously, many people in the church have taken a passive role when it comes to healing. You often hear statements like: "If the Lord chooses to manifest healing," or, "This person really operates in the gift of healing." Usually these types of statements originate from wrong teaching and/or ignorance concerning the Scriptures. I think it would be advantageous for us to examine the gift of healing in further detail. The Bible tells us:

> *Now there are diversities of gifts, but the same Spirit. And there are differences of administrations, but the same Lord. And there are diversities of operations, but it is the same God which worketh all in all. But the* **manifestation** *of the Spirit is given to every man to profit withal* (1 Corinthians 12:4-7).

Here we see that gifts (or manifestations) are given by the Holy Spirit for the collective benefit of the body of Christ. In the case of healing, the Holy Spirit manifests the gift of healing through an individual, group of people, or in an atmosphere. This gift usually operates independently from a person's faith. A great example of this would be the man at the pool of Bethesda found in John's gospel account.

> *Jesus saith unto him, Rise, take up thy bed, and walk. And immediately the man was made whole, and took up his bed, and walked: and on the same day was the sabbath* (John 5:8-9).

If you pay close attention to the text, you will notice that this man did not have faith to receive healing. In fact, when Jesus asked him the profound question, "Wilt thou be made whole?" the impotent man responded with a series of excuses (no help getting into the pool, prolonged illness, etc.). This miraculous manifestation rested solely on Jesus as the Healer (*Jehovah Rapha*) and not the faith of the man receiving the miracle.

Though this passage is not specifically related to spiritual gifts, it gives us great insight into the way the Holy Spirit manifests the gift of healing. The operative word is *gift*. There are times in a service when the Holy Spirit may give a specific word of knowledge concerning a physical ailment accompanied by a physical manifestation of healing. This manifestation is usually spontaneous in nature, and can come through whomever God decides to use in that moment. It is prompted by the Spirit Himself and has nothing to do with the thoughts, desires, or inherent spirituality of the vessel involved, although faith is required to believe the Holy Spirit to do the manifesting.

One time, I was in a healing service and I heard the Spirit say, "I am healing knees right now," so I spoke this out to the congregation. All of a sudden, people came forward testifying that their knees had been healed instantly. This was a manifestation of the gift of healing through a particular vessel at a particular time (myself in that instance). I never planned or arranged for this to happen. It had nothing to do with my faith or spirituality; it was simply a manifestation of the Holy Spirit to heal those who were being afflicted by that specific condition. The more we are sensitive to the Holy Spirit, the more He is able to operate through us freely and manifest various gifts—specifically healing. You will notice that there are people in the church who seem to manifest healing to a greater degree or more frequently than others. Many times this is due to the unique operation of the Spirit through that individual or group of people. This can also be a result of the person being more sensitive to the Spirit's leading at any given time. However, we all can walk in divine healing to a greater degree as our faith, expectation, and spiritual activity increase.

THE RESPONSIBILITY TO HEAL

And these signs shall follow them that believe; in my name shall they cast out devils; they shall speak with new tongues; they shall take up serpents; and if they drink any deadly thing, it shall not hurt them; they shall lay hands on the sick, and they shall recover (Mark 16:17-18).

Greater than the gift of healing is the Christian responsibility to heal the sick.

The Bible tells us in Mark 16:18, "they shall lay hands on the sick and they shall recover." We mentioned before that this is a promise from Jesus Himself. It is a guarantee!

Unlike the gift of healing, this is not about some spontaneous manifestation of the Spirit or about a particular vessel through whom God operates; this is the divine mandate for every single believer. Every believer is called by Jesus Christ to heal the sick, among other things. We don't have to wait for a fuzzy feeling or a prophetic word; whenever or wherever there is sickness, you and I have been given the authority, the power, and the responsibility to heal.

The Bible says, "These signs shall follow them that believe" (Mark 16:17) Notice the Bible did not say, "These signs shall follow those who possess the gift of healing," or, "These signs shall follow those who are specially anointed by God to heal." The prerequisite for healing is *believing*. What does it mean to believe? To believe simply means to accept something as the truth. When you accept something as the truth, you embrace it; and when you embrace, it you act on it!

It is said that action activates miracles. This is a very true statement. When we recognize our responsibility to heal the sick according to the Word of God, we will stop waiting for someone else to do it and start acting on the truth. For instance, if there is someone in your church, small group, or community dealing with a physical illness—lay hands on him or her and pray for them. Don't hold off until reinforcements show up! Pray for the person now! They may not be able to wait until "Sister Super Saint" comes to pray for them. Healing is the children's bread. It is a covenant right that we possess as a result of the redemptive sacrifice of Jesus. Even if you don't feel anointed, pray anyway! The power will show up later. The key is knowing what your rights and responsibilities are under the New Covenant. I can't tell you how many times I have prayed for people and I didn't feel a thing. Now I recognize that healing is not a feeling, it is a spiritual reality based on the atonement.

Every believer has been commissioned to heal the sick as an expression of God's Kingdom.

This kind of thinking flies in the face of religion and tradition, but make no mistake—it is absolutely biblical. In my book, *The Power of Unlimited Faith*, I talk about the supernatural power of God that is released when you and I take the limits off our faith and expectation. I believe that many people are not seeing the miraculous manifestation of healing because they refuse to believe God and act on His Word. It has nothing to do with whether or not the gifts of the Spirit are in operation. That, my friend, is a religious excuse! There was only one instance in the Bible where Jesus was restricted in His ability to manifest healing (at least to the degree He desired)—when the people refused to believe. The Bible says:

> *But Jesus said unto them, A prophet is not without honour, but in his own country, and among his own kin, and in his own house. And he could there*

do no mighty work, save that he laid his hands upon a few sick folk, and healed them. And he marvelled because of their unbelief. And he went round about the villages, teaching (Mark 6:4-6).

Notice that the Bible says, "And he could there do no mighty work." This is how it is expressed in the Amplified Bible:

And He was not able to do even one work of power there, except that He laid His hands on a few sickly people [and] cured them (Mark 6:5 AMP).

Notice that the Bible says that Jesus could not heal or manifest miracles to the degree He intended because of the unbelief of the people. Unbelief inhibits the full manifestation of healing. I want to emphasize the word *full*. Jesus still healed people, but it was not the fullness of His power. In other words, it was limited! Jesus never once said, "I can't heal people because the Holy Spirit is not operating in that way."

Some of you may be thinking, "But He was Jesus; He didn't need the Holy Spirit!" You would be absolutely wrong! Every healing miracle Jesus performed was accomplished through the power and anointing of the Holy Spirit; the same Holy Spirit who lives and dwells in you as a born-again believer.

It is time for the church to stand up and move in the power and authority that God gave us. For instance, if a person was possessed with a demon spirit, you wouldn't sit around and wait for a deliverance minister or someone with the "gift of deliverance" to walk in the room—or at least you shouldn't. You would take authority over the powers of darkness in Jesus's name. Why? You have the power and the authority to address the demonic attack.

> *Because of the indwelling Christ, we have both the right and the responsibility to heal.*

Our responsibility to heal the sick is no different. Who-ever has been given the authority has also been given the responsibility. Can you imagine a police officer watching a crime transpire and refusing to act? It is almost incom-prehensible, isn't it? The moment that officer received his badge, he took on the responsibility to uphold the law as much as possible. In the same way, you have been deputized in the Kingdom of God as an agent of healing and resto-ration to everyone around you. Whether or not you possess the "gift of healing" is irrelevant. Furthermore, the gift of healing does not have a patent on it. The Holy Spirit can manifest healing through anyone He chooses. We have to change our thinking when it comes to the subject of heal-ing. The power to heal does not rest in a personality or a denomination. We can't package it and sell it as if it is some product or service. Once you understand this, you will stop being passive and get involved in the Kingdom mandate to advance God's healing agenda in the earth.

SUMMARY QUESTIONS

1. What is the biblical definition of the "gift of healing" according to First Corinthians 12?

2. How do spiritual gifts operate?

3. What is the difference between the gift of healing and the mandate to heal?

4. What is the only thing listed in the Bible that kept healing from manifesting in its fullness?

CHAPTER 8

HEALING PRACTICUM

And heal the sick that are therein, and say unto them, The kingdom of God is come nigh unto you (Luke 10:9).

I absolutely love Luke's gospel! In it we find a very detailed account of several healing miracles. Scholars agree that there are more healing miracles in the book of Luke than any other gospel, probably due to the fact that Luke was a physician by trade. As a physician, he must have been highly fascinated with healing. I believe that God sovereignly used Luke's personality and medical interest to express the healing power of God in this gospel account. Though I am not a physician, I share Luke's sentiment. Healing is a wonderful display of God's goodness and compassion toward us. What an awesome God we serve!

I believe that there are some very practical things you and I can learn when it comes to ministering healing to others. The first practical step is to actually go out and heal the sick. That's right! I said *go out* and heal the sick. Many people are waiting for some angelic voice to speak to them and say: "Thus saith the Lord: I have chosen you as a vessel of healing; now go wherever I shall send thee." I am sure some people have had this kind of miraculous "mountain-top experience," but most have not. Healing is not mystical at all. In fact, healing is very pragmatic in nature. Why? Because the physical manifestation of healing serves as the sign or proof that the person has received something super-natural in their physical body.

Oftentimes when I am ministering healing to others, I will ask them to confirm their healing in some tangible or practical way. For example, if a person has an issue of chronic back pain and they come for healing, I will often ask them to do something physically that they were pre-viously restricted from doing as a result of the pain. This serves as the practical manifestation of their healing. Other times, I will ask a person to confirm the healing miracle with their doctor. Please don't misunderstand me—I believe that people are healed regardless of what they feel, but it is good to make a habit of addressing the practical side of heal-ing as well. Jesus modeled this type of ministry in the gospel accounts. The Bible says:

> *And he cometh to Bethsaida; and they bring a blind man unto him, and besought him to touch him. And he took the blind man by the hand, and led him out of the town; and when he had spit on his eyes, and put his hands upon him, he asked*

him if he saw ought. And he looked up, and said,
I see men as trees, walking. After that he put his
hands again upon his eyes, and made him look up:
and he was restored, and saw every man clearly
(Mark 8:22-25).

In the Gospel of Mark, Jesus came across a blind man. Unlike many encounters with the sick, Jesus resorted to a very hands-on approach to this healing miracle. In this particular instance, Jesus spit on the blind man's eyes. I don't know if this would be well received in our modern times! After He spit on the blind man's eyes, He asked him if he saw anything. To this, the blind man responded, "I see men as trees walking." Apparently there was need for more healing.

The ultimate goal is to bring the person you are praying for to a place of healing and wholeness.

Notice that Jesus asked for feedback while He prayed for this man afflicted with blindness. This is very important. Why? Because there should be tangible results when you pray for the sick. Jesus did not say, "Oh well, at least it's better!" Instead, He worked with the blind man until he was completely restored. This might be considered a progressive healing. Jesus, the Creator of the Universe, did not mind praying for the man a second time. How amazing is that! I am sure this miracle could have taken place instantly, but I believe there is a lesson to be learned. Healing ministry is hands on! It will require that we get our hands dirty, so to speak, and persevere until we see breakthrough—especially when we first begin.

For this reason, many pastors are not interested in healing in their church, because they simply don't want to deal with the "mess" and the "liability." The truth is that the liability of healing does not rest upon us, but on Jesus Christ Himself. There are times when you may be praying for someone and they may tell you that they are not feeling any better; keep going until they do. Don't be discouraged! This will build your faith and endurance for the next situation you encounter. I believe that many people don't receive their healing because church people are often lazy. They are unwilling to persevere until they see breakthrough. The key is actually going and ministering to the sick. If you don't know where to start, begin with people in your local church (with your pastor's permission) or the local hospitals. As long as you operate according to the Word of God and the leading of the Holy Spirit, you will be just fine. Remember, it is not about you; it is about Him and them.

PRACTICING SPIRITUAL SENSITIVITY

And it came to pass on a certain day, as he was teaching, that there were Pharisees and doctors of the law sitting by, which were come out of every town of Galilee, and Judaea, and Jerusalem: and the power of the Lord was present to heal them (Luke 5:17).

As you continue to move forward in your pursuit of a consistent lifestyle of healing the sick, it is important to develop a practice of being sensitive to the Holy Spirit. Contrary to conventional thinking, healing miracles do not have to only take place in a church setting. In fact, most healing miracles recorded in the gospel accounts took place outside the four walls of the synagogue (which was equivalent to the church at that time). Jesus understood this profound reality. He constantly discerned the presence and power of God in various situations.

In Luke 5:17, Jesus was teaching and sensed the healing power of God was present to heal. The word *present* is from a Greek preposition that denotes "unto or toward." What is the significance of this word? Jesus recognized that the miracle-working power of God was moving in the direction of healing. The power was "pointing" toward healing. The atmosphere was literally charged with the *dynamis* power of God.

As the account continues, Jesus encountered a man with palsy and healed him of the infirmity. The idea is that Jesus didn't just continue to teach once He sensed that there was a shift in the atmosphere; He shifted into demonstration once He recognized that the supernatural healing power of God was in manifestation. There are times when I may be teaching a message, and I discern that the power of God is present to heal, and I shift from teaching to ministering healing. There are other times when I am walking in a grocery store and the Holy Spirit will impress upon my heart the unction to lay hands on people in the store. The key is sensitivity. This sensitivity not only includes the ability to recognize the healing power of God in manifestation, but also the ability to know how to minister to different people in different scenarios. For instance, there was a situation where a woman came to me for prayer during a healing service, and as I was about to lay hands on her to pray I sensed that the Holy Spirit did not want me to lay hands, but to speak the Word instead. That is exactly what I did, and the woman was supernaturally healed instantly. Praise the Lord! Many times, I have no idea why the Holy Spirit will direct me in a certain way, but I know that every time I follow His leading it produces the best outcome.

The more sensitive you are in discerning the activity of the Holy Spirit, the more effective you will become in healing the sick.

JUST DO IT!

Many of you reading this book may be familiar with the famous Nike slogan "Just do it!" There could not be a more apt expression when it comes to healing the sick. Ultimately, we just have to do it. When my sister was in medical school, she was required to do what was known as a residency; this involved working in a clinical environment among patients and fellow caregivers. The idea was to allow students to gain firsthand experience with the real world and put into practice the things they learned in an academic setting. You and

I have to put healing to practice. We have to "just do it!" Some may ask, "How do I do that?" As I mentioned earlier, many healing encounters take place outside of the four walls of the church; this is why everyday scenarios are a great starting place. To illustrate this point, I will share with you a testimony.

HEALING TESTIMONY

One day on a Sunday afternoon, my wife and I encountered a woman in a gift shop who was suffering from severe back pain. My wife engaged in several conversations with this lady as we frequented this particular gift shop. This lady told my wife that she did not believe in God and she did not believe in healing. She thought that healing ministers were charlatans who were simply out to take people's hard-earned money. However, she knew that my wife was a believer and asked her to pray for her back. My wife later informed me that there was a lady who requested prayer, and we proceeded to the gift shop.

As we entered the shop, she was literally bowed over in pain. I asked her what the problem was, and she told me that she was suffering from a slipped disk in her back and that the pain was unbearable. I asked her if she believed that Jesus could heal her. She then stared at me with a suspicious gaze and said, "If you say so!" She clearly didn't believe in Jesus or healing.

Then I asked her, "If Jesus touched your back and healed you, would you believe?"

She said, "Maybe, but nothing is going to happen!"

I was up for the challenge. In fact, these types of scenarios are great platforms for healing miracles. Remember, the greater the challenge, the greater the miracle. I told her that Jesus was about to show her just how real He is. I laid hands on her shoulder (after asking permission to do so) and began to pray. I spoke to the spinal cord, muscular system, and nervous system and commanded the pain to go immediately. Then I said, "Jesus, show her how real You are!"

After I prayed for the woman, I looked at her and asked what took place in her body, and she said, "You are going to think I am crazy, but the pain went away completely." She was still a bit skeptical so I began to prophesy over her and speak words of knowledge. I told her about her childhood and other details in her life. This lady was instantly healed and astonished by the power of God. Notice, I couldn't wait for flashy lights or worship music; I simply acted in faith and prayed for the sick. As a result, God met us at the very point of our expectation. I just did it!

The more we place a demand on God's power, the more He will manifest Himself on our behalf.

Why was this encounter so important? Why was it necessary to heal this woman outside the confines of the church? It is quite simple! God wanted to show her that He was real. He did not want her to be distracted by the lights, hype, or religious jargon (though I love when healing takes place in church). Jesus manifested Himself in an unconventional way, through an unconventional encounter, in an unconventional environment. The key is to get out and do it. Go to your nearest college or university and offer to pray for the sick. This is also an excellent way to share your faith. There are people in the world today who will not step foot in a church building; therefore, we have to take God's healing power to them. This is what Jesus intended when He said:

> *And into whatsoever city ye enter, and they receive you, eat such things as are set before you: and heal the sick that are therein, and say unto them, The kingdom of God is come nigh unto you* (Luke 10:8-9).

Jesus said that we should say "the Kingdom has come to you." What did He mean by this statement? He means that you have come to the person in need of the miracle. You are a carrier of the Kingdom of God on the inside of you. This is why, whenever you enter a building or come into an environment, the Kingdom of God has come to that place. Get into the habit of seeing things from this vantage point. As we mentioned previously, you have the authority of the Lord Jesus Christ on the inside of you. Don't be afraid! Be bold! Don't worry about how things will turn out. Simply take action in faith, and the Holy Spirit will take care of the rest.

PRACTICAL APPLICATION

For this chapter, it's time to let the rubber meet the road!

1. If you have never prayed for healing before, ask God's forgiveness for any laziness that may have prevented you. Ask Him to give you divine courage to release healing, if you have struggled with fear.

2. Ask God to supply you with a "divine appointment" today. Prepare by listening to the Holy Spirit, and tell Him that you commit to pray for the person He will point out.

3. Just do it! When you feel the Holy Spirit leading you to pray for a sick person, step out and pray! Remember, healing is a Kingdom reality you carry within you. Release it and allow God to work.

4. Thank God for using you as His hands and feet. Ask Him to prepare another "divine appointment" for you tomorrow!

CHAPTER 9

PRAYING FOR THE SICK

And the prayer of faith shall save the sick, and the Lord shall raise him up; and if he have committed sins, they shall be forgiven him (James 5:15).

Whether you realize it or not, prayer is very powerful. Prayer is especially effective in ministering to the sick. I believe that the church, for the most part, has been negligent of the profound power of prayer. We often see it as a last resort in desperate situations or some religious obligation. Beloved, prayer is so much more than that! The question is, how do we pray for the sick? Is there a right and wrong way to pray? Are there prerequisites for praying for the sick? These are all very important questions as we pursue a consistent lifestyle of healing the sick.

The Bible says that the "prayer of faith" will save the sick. What does this mean? The first thing that we should do is define prayer. The word for *prayer* found in James 5:15

is the Greek word *euchē*, which simply means to communicate with God. Essentially prayer is the means by which we communicate with God and invite His divine presence and power in our natural affairs. Prayer comes in many forms, but at its core prayer is an invocation. What does that mean? Every time we pray, we are inviting God to move in and on our behalf, or on the behalf of others. What does this have to do with healing? Divine healing is supernatural, and if we are going to walk in divine healing and/or minister healing to others, we need to learn to tap in to God's supernatural power. The primary means of doing this is prayer. In fact, secular research even acknowledges the tangible effect of prayer on the sick. According to an article by the American Cancer Society:

> Research has also been conducted on the effects of intercessory prayer in coronary care patients. In the late 1980s, a study in San Francisco reported that heart patients who were prayed for by others appeared to have fewer complications, although length of hospital stay and death rates did not differ between those who were prayed for and those who were not. A larger study at a Kansas City hospital coronary care unit reported similar findings. Although overall length of hospital stay and time in the critical care unit did not differ between groups, the group that had been prayed for had 11% fewer complications. These results suggested that prayer might be helpful when used

with conventional medical care, although more research was needed to be sure.[1]

THE PRAYER OF FAITH

I am by no means suggesting that prayer needs to be validated or endorsed by the medical community, but I do believe that it is an interesting example of the effect prayer (in general) has on the secular medical community. Regardless of what scientists say, prayer has been God's divine tool of choice to affect change in the lives of His children since the beginning of time. The Bible says that the prayer of faith will *save* the sick. If this is the case, then why don't we pray for the sick more often?

There are several reasons why we don't pray for the sick the way we should, but I believe the most glaring is the fact that many people do not know how to pray. It is very difficult to do something you don't know how to do. The Bible qualifies the type of prayer we should be engaged in when it comes to ministering to the sick—the prayer of faith. The key word is *faith*. We will talk more about faith in a later chapter, but I want to emphasize the importance of praying in faith according to the will of God. What is the will of God? The Word of God! God's Word says that He desires the sick to be healed. If He didn't want the sick to be healed, then why would He command us to pray for the sick? The truth is that God not only desires, He longs for the sick to be healed. We must pray with the resolve in our heart that God desires to raise up the person we are praying for from their bed of affliction, by His power.

Oftentimes, when I hear people praying for the sick, I notice that they are doing more begging and crying than praying. "Lord, if it be Thy holy will, look down upon this poor lowly soul and comfort them in their ailment." It seems as if they are eulogizing the sick person in advance. This is the wrong way to pray! Why? It is not according to the will of God. I often tell people that if they are going to pray that way, please do not bother to pray for me or anyone else. Don't misunderstand me—there is nothing wrong with crying out to God in prayer, but that is totally different from the defeated prayers that many people pray.

> *Prayer releases God's divine power and invokes His presence in our natural affairs.*

Years ago, I was attending a church Bible study, and the pastor said the most awful thing I had ever heard. He said that Isaiah 53:5, which says, "But he was wounded for our transgressions, he was bruised for our iniquities: the chastisement of our peace was upon him; and with his stripes we are healed," was not at all referring to physical healing. I wondered in my mind what else it could possibly be talking about. While confused and troubled, I asked the pastor, "Well then, what do you pray when a person is sick?"

He responded by saying, "I pray that God comforts them!" I was absolutely horrified by this response. It was then that I realized that some people have no business praying for the sick. They are actually agreeing with Satan to kill the person being prayed for. Beloved, God has something so much better in store for us. He wants us to know that *it is His unconditional will to heal the sick.* Now that you know this, you can approach prayer from a totally different paradigm.

THE POWER OF EFFECTUAL PRAYER

The Bible tells us in James 5 that the prayer of faith will save the sick. Notice the emphasis on salvation. Why didn't the Bible say, "Heal the sick"? I go into great detail about this in my book *Possessing Your Healing*, but it would suffice to say that sickness is evil. This is one of the greatest revelations I have come to in my personal life. The enemy uses sickness to enslave people and discourage them from worshiping God in spirit and truth. Therefore, the prayer of faith literally "saves" the sick. This is the Greek word *sozo*; incidentally, the same word for salvation found in Romans 10:8-10. It means to rescue from evil or danger. It also carries with it the connotation of healing, restoration, wholeness, and safety. Through the power of prayer, the sick are restored to a place of healing and wholeness.

Earlier, we posed the question, "What are the prerequisites for praying for the sick?" The first thing that we mentioned was faith. The Bible explicitly states that it is the prayer of faith that brings salvation, healing, and restoration to the person being afflicted by sickness. What does this look like? In the very next verse, the Bible tells us how we ought to pray.

> *Confess your faults one to another, and pray one for another, that ye may be healed. The effectual fervent prayer of a righteous man availeth much* (James 5:16).

What does the Bible mean when it says, "The effectual fervent prayer of a righteous man availeth much"? The words *effectual* and *fervent* both come from the Greek word *energeo* (Strong's, G1754), which means "to put forth power or to be operative." It is where we get the English word *energy*. Energy is defined as the strength and vitality required for sustained physical or mental activity. In the case of prayer, we must exert energy or spiritual power in order to affect change in the spiritual and physical realm. The Bible says that it is the "effectual and fervent prayer" (i.e. energetic, passionate, and heartfelt prayer) that will produce results. Here is how it is expressed in the Amplified Bible:

> *The earnest (heartfelt, continued) prayer of a righteous man makes tremendous power available [dynamic in its working].*

Isn't that just amazing? We are not to pray apathetic, lifeless prayers. Many believers are praying this way and frustrated that they are not seeing any results. They say, "Oh well, it must not have been God's will to heal that person!" I believe that this is simply another religious excuse. These are what I call "lazy prayers." We often pray with a lack of enthusiasm and zeal when we secretly believe nothing will happen or if we have a "plan B" in place. Beloved, in the Kingdom of God, there is no plan B. I often wonder how many people have been overtaken by sickness even to the point of death because the church at large has been apathetic toward sickness. Beloved, we must stop making excuses and start fighting for our healing and the healing of others. The Bible says, "pray for one another." This is an act of love and compassion. Are you willing to labor for your brother or sister in prayer until they see breakthrough? This is an absolute necessity in consistently seeing the sick healed.

HEALING TESTIMONY

Many years ago, my wife and I were at home with our children, and we noticed that our eldest daughter was beginning to come down with a fever. As I laid my hands on her head, I noticed that her temperature was extremely high. When we took her temperature, it was over 104 degrees Fahrenheit. Her entire body became hot, and she began to scream in pain. At the time we didn't know what to do. My first thought was to rush her to the emergency room. There is nothing like watching your children suffer in pain and agony. Being the people of faith we are, we started praying. We rebuked the fever and declared her healing. The more we prayed for her, the more she cried in pain. The situation seemed to be getting worse!

It is one thing to minister healing to people outside your home, but a completely different thing altogether to minister healing to your own family. "What are we going to do?" I thought.

The prayers of the righteous are highly effective even in the most impossible situations.

My wife and I decided to see this thing through in prayer. We told our daughter to pray, "Jesus, thank You for healing me!" She prayed this precious prayer several times. Right when I was ready to give up on prayer and seek alternative care, the Lord spoke to my inner man. I remembered that the effectual and fervent prayer of the righteous was highly effective. I realized that prayer works, no matter the situation. My wife and I put our foot to the grindstone and we began waging holy war on that ungodly fever. In the space of about fifteen minutes, my daughter vomited on the floor, and shortly after that the fever was broken. My daughter looked up at us and said, "I am hungry." She was completely healed in Jesus's name!

The purpose of this testimony is not to suggest that you shouldn't take your children to the doctor, but to emphasize the supernatural power of persistent, heartfelt prayer. What would happen if you and I applied this kind of relentless zeal every time we prayed?

THE LABOR ROOM

When my wife was pregnant with our first child, she went through many complications. Thankfully, most of them were mild, but irritating nonetheless. Toward the latter part of her pregnancy, the doctors decided that my daughter ran the risk of being a high birth weight baby. According to conventional medicine, the larger the child, the greater the risk of labor complications and the need for a C-section. My wife and I decided toward the beginning of the pregnancy that she would not undergo a C-section, so the suggestions to do so by her OB/GYN were firmly rejected. Now we were nine months into the pregnancy and expecting my daughter any moment. The next thing we knew we were in the labor room for a scheduled induction. The problem was that my wife's cervix refused to dilate; this caused a very prolonged and painful labor. The doctor came in the room and told us that she would be forced to perform a C-section because my wife was not making enough progress (dilation) for a natural birth.

This was not the news that we wanted to hear. We begged her to reconsider. The doctor said that she would give us a little more time, and if my wife still wasn't dilated she would have to proceed with the C-section. After several hours my wife was barely two centimeters dilated (this was not even close to the nine to ten centimeters necessary for a healthy natural delivery). We began praying over her body. The doctor came in yet again with a negative report. She said that she would have to perform the C-section and we had one hour, during which time she would prepare for the operation. They were concerned for the baby's health. One hour! That was all the time we had left for a miracle, and things weren't looking good at all. Unfortunately for the devil, I am no quitter. Now it was personal!

In my righteous indignation I began to come against Satan with all of my heart and soul. I started to talk to my wife's stomach. I told my unborn daughter that it was time to come out now. By this time my wife was asleep, exhausted by the intense labor. I prayed in tongues over her stomach for an hour. All of a sudden, she began contracting. When the doctor walked in and checked my wife for dilation, she screamed, "The head is coming out!" She told me to put on my gloves and come quickly. Minutes later, my wife gave birth to our oldest daughter—beautiful Immanuella Bridges. Hallelujah!

Prayer is the labor room of the miraculous! Keep praying until you give birth to your miracle.

The reason I share this very personal testimony is to illustrate the power of prayer and teach you that we must labor in prayer if we want to see the manifestation of God's power in our lives. In fact, I would say that prayer is the labor room of the miraculous. What do I mean by this expression? While my wife was going through intense labor in order to give birth to our daughter, we were also laboring spiritually in prayer to give birth to the miracle we were believing God to manifest. Too many people give up on prayer too soon. This is not the will of God, my friend! He wants us to keep interceding in the Spirit until we see manifestation. This is very true of divine healing. In Matthew, the Bible says:

> *Ask, and it shall be given you; seek, and ye shall find; knock, and it shall be opened unto you: for every one that asketh receiveth; and he that seeketh findeth; and to him that knocketh it shall be opened* (Matthew 7:7-8).

Most people interpret this verse to mean, "Ask one time and if it is God's will it will happen immediately." That is not what the Word of God says at all. In fact, this is written in the perpetual tense. In other words, "Keep on asking and it will be given you; keep on seeking and you will find; keep on knocking [reverently] and [the door] will be opened to you" (Matt. 7:7 AMP). The key is relentlessness. The Kingdom of God is not for the faint at heart, but for those who will refuse to accept "No" for an answer. Make up your mind that you will see the sick healed, because it is the will of God. To be clear, I am not referring to praying out of fear or doubt, but I am talking about an attitude of faith that refuses to give up until it receives what God has promised.

PRAYING ACCORDING TO GOD'S WILL

And this is the confidence that we have in him, that, if we ask any thing according to his will, he heareth us (1 John 5:14).

It is very important that we understand the necessity of praying according to the will of God. The Bible tells us in First John that if we ask anything according to the will of God, He hears us. Isn't this great news? The term *will* comes from the Greek word *thelēma*, which means "what one wishes or has determined shall be done." The Bible says that God works all things after the counsel of His own will (see Eph. 1:11). What is the counsel of God's will? Psalm 138:2 says, "I will worship toward thy holy temple, and praise thy name for thy lovingkindness and for thy truth: for thou hast magnified thy word above all thy name." Simply put, God's will is His written and revealed Word. This is the counsel by which God governs Himself and all of creation. The Word of God reveals the heart of God—His purposes, desires, and intentions.

If only the church realized that the Word of God was the will of God, then we would pray according to the Word. When we pray according to God's Word, we are guaranteed to see victory. The question remains—what is God's will concerning sickness? Healing! The Bible tells us in Acts 10:38 that God anointed Jesus of Nazareth with the Holy Ghost, who went about doing good, healing *all* who were oppressed of the devil. I want to put special emphasis on the word *all*. If Jesus went about doing good and healing *all*, then we ought to be engaged in the same mission (see John 14:12).

We must learn to pray according to the perfect will of God if we want to get results.

We ought to pray that the sick be healed, that the lame walk, and that blind eyes are opened; this is the perfect will of God. I believe the reason why many prayers are not answered is due to the fact that they do not align with the will of God. For example, a person receives a terminal diagnosis, and they share this news with other believers in their church or spiritual community, hoping their community will wage holy war against their affliction; instead, people often exacerbate the situation by praying prayers that aid and abet sickness. "Please Lord, let Your will be done in sister so and so's life," or, "Lord, give them the strength to bear this thorn in their flesh." On the surface this seems like a fairly pious prayer right? Wrong! This type of prayer is rooted in fear, doubt, and unbelief rather than faith and confidence in God's Word. These are what I call "insurance policy prayers." We pray these kinds of prayers when we are not sure what God's will is or what the outcome will be. "Lord whether You heal them or call them home, You decide!"

At the risk of sounding offensive, I beg you to consider what God's Word says about sickness. There is never a question whether or not God desires to heal one of His children. Healing is necessary for this life, not when we get to heaven.

That is simply an oxymoronic prayer. When we pray with that kind of doubt and uncertainty, we are almost guaranteed to get a less than favorable outcome. Imagine a husband and wife going through difficulty saying, "If we make or if we fail, God's will be done!" That marriage is bound to fail. The only way for a marriage succeed is the determination, "No matter what, we will do what it takes to make this marriage work." The same is true of healing!

OVERCOMING THE DOUBLE MIND

A double minded man is unstable in all his ways (James 1:8).

In my experience with healing ministry, there is nothing more counterproductive (and often damaging) than being double-minded in prayer. The Bible says in James 1:6-7, "But let him ask in faith, nothing wavering. For he that wavereth is like a wave of the sea driven with the wind and tossed. *For let not that man think that he shall receive any thing of the Lord.*" Notice that the Bible says that we are not to ask and waver. What does it mean to waver? The term *waver* comes from the Greek word *diakrinō*, which means "to be at variance with one's self, hesitate, or doubt." In other words, whenever we are wavering we are at variance or opposition with ourselves.

How does this relate to praying for the sick? You cannot pray for the sick to be healed while at the same time afraid that they will not be healed. You cannot declare life while anticipating death. This is what the Bible calls being double minded. If you are operating in this kind of mentality, the Bible says that you are like a wave of the sea, driven of the wind and tossed. Have you ever seen a wave in the ocean? It is extremely unpredictable. You have no idea where it is going to go next or what it is going to do. So is the person operating with a double mind. They are operating in doubt and unbelief. The term *double mind* comes from the Greek word *dipsychos*, which means "divided mind or two minds." If you are going to be effective in healing the sick, you must be single-minded. You must make up your mind that it is the unconditional will of God to heal the sick, and act on that biblical truth until you see it manifest. Don't vacillate back and forth between faith and fear!

> *Praying with a double mind will always block your ability to receive answered prayer.*

Many years ago, I was double-minded. I thought that God's will varied depending on the circumstances that I faced. This was my reality until the Word of God became the final authority in my life. The Word of God must become the final authority in your life before you will ever really experience breakthrough, especially as it relates to divine healing. People often attempt to come up with scenarios where the Word of God does not work, whether it is in their finances, health, marriage, or ministry. Beloved, there is absolutely no scenario where the Word of God doesn't work. Don't listen to the lies of the enemy. The devil doesn't want you to receive the answers to your prayer, so he attempts to discourage you through situations, circumstances, and people. Don't give in to his lies! Make the quality decision today to settle your heart and mind on the truth of the Word.

We have to come to a place where God's Word is true and everything and everyone else is a liar. This will never happen if you refuse to admit that you are the problem and not God. He is always right! Be single-minded today and you will reap the benefits of answered prayer and a life of miracles.

PRAYING FOR SPECIFIC AILMENTS

The more you minister to the sick, the more you will learn how to identify specific ailments or disease clusters. I have learned that there are certain physiological root causes to certain conditions. It is important to become familiar with human anatomy as you grow in your understanding of healing. This will help you to identify certain conditions and become more effective in praying for those conditions. Below is a basic diagram of the human body:

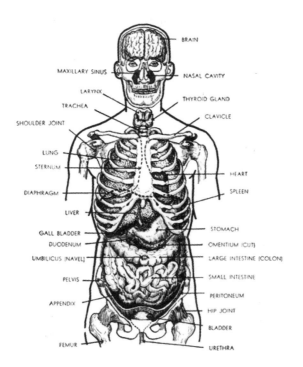

Based on our knowledge of the human body, we are empowered to "target" our prayers for maximum impact. Below are a few examples of chronic conditions and how to pray for them.

1. **Gout:** Inflammation and pain due to uric acid buildup in the body; therefore we pray: *"Father, in Jesus's name, I command the excess acid to leave and for the inflammation to go now!"*

2. **Lupus:** Autoimmune disorder: *"Father, in the name of Jesus, I command the immune system to*

come into divine order and for all pain, inflammation, and bruising to cease and desist, right now!"

3. **Cancer:** Rapid duplication of abnormal cells: *"Father, we curse the cancerous cells and command them to die and healthy cells to regenerate in Jesus's name."*

4. **Crohn's Disease:** Inflammation in the intestines: *"Father, in Jesus's name, I speak to the small intestines, large intestines, and colon and command them to come into alignment and order in Jesus's name. We command pain and inflammation to cease now!"*

This is by no means an exhaustive list, but a great starting place in learning how to pray specific prayers for healing specific chronic conditions. Remember, practice makes permanent!

HEALING PRAYER

Father, in the name of Jesus Christ, I thank You for Your goodness and grace. I thank You that Your will is always to heal the sick. According to Your Word, I commit myself to pray for the sick regularly, and by Your grace and power I will see the sick restored to health and the dead raised to life in Jesus's name! I refuse to be afraid of not receiving the answer to my prayers, because I know how to pray according to

Your perfect will. Your Word is Your will; therefore I have confidence that as I pray Your Word, I will always see Kingdom results in my life and the lives of those I pray for. In Jesus's name! Amen.

SUMMARY QUESTIONS

1. What is the most effective way to pray for the sick?

2. What does the Bible mean by the term "effectual and fervent" prayer?

3. What does the Bible promise to those who pray according to God's will?

4. What is the number-one barrier to answered prayer?

NOTE

1. Herbert Benson, et al., "Study of the Therapeutic Effects of Intercessory Prayer (STEP) in Cardiac Bypass Patients," *American Heart Journal* 151, no. 4 (2006): 934-942, doi:10.1016/j.ahj.2005.05.028.

CHAPTER 10

HEALING AND CONFESSION

Death and life are in the power of the tongue: and they that love it shall eat the fruit thereof (Proverbs 18:21).

By now I think it is safe to say that you have resolved within yourself that healing is the will of God. If my assumption is correct, then it is important to understand yet another critical component to receiving and ministering healing—our words! You may be wondering what our words have to do with healing, but I would suggest that the words we speak or confess have a profound effect on our ability to walk in health and healing. The Bible declares that death and life are in the power of the tongue. The Bible goes further to say that those who love it shall eat its fruit (see Prov. 18:21).

What in heaven does that mean? Simply put, your mouth is a divine orifice, capable of releasing both life and death, sickness and healing. Whatever comes out of our mouth consistently will become the fruit from which

we partake. Ironically, many believers are ignorant and/
or negligent of this spiritual principle. I cannot tell you the
countless times I have witnessed Christians violate this principle and speak death over themselves and others. Due to
the power of our words, our consistent confession is a very
important dynamic when it comes to divine healing. The
Bible says this:

> That if thou shalt confess with thy mouth the
> Lord Jesus, and shalt believe in thine heart that
> God hath raised him from the dead, thou shalt be
> saved. For with the heart man believeth unto righ-
> teousness; and with the mouth confession is made
> unto salvation (Romans 10:9-10).

Here in Romans 10, the Bible says that if we confess
with our mouth and believe in our heart, we shall be
saved. The context of this passage is God's plan for Israel
and eternal salvation; however, we mentioned earlier that
the term *salvation* (*sozo*) is an all-encompassing word
which includes health and healing. Notice that the vehicle
for this salvation is confession. The Bible says, "confession
is made unto salvation." What does it mean to confess?
The word *confession* found in Romans 10 comes from the
Greek word *homologeō*, which means "to say what has
already been said, to say the same thing as another, and
to declare openly." From a biblical standpoint, confession
is the act of saying or declaring the same thing that God
says. When we learn to proclaim God's Word rather than
what we think, see, or feel, we are engaging in the practice

of biblical confession. Why is this so important? That which you confess and believe, you will ultimately receive.

CONFESSION = POSSESSION

*For verily I say unto you, That whosoever shall say unto this mountain, Be thou removed, and be thou cast into the sea; and shall not doubt in his heart, but shall believe that those things which **he saith** shall come to pass; he shall have **whatsoever he saith*** (Mark 11:23).

The Bible is very clear as it relates to the power of confessing the Word. Regardless of what you have been told, confessing the Word of God over your life and circumstances is a very important key to experiencing God's miracle power. Those who choose to obey this spiritual law will reap its benefits, and those who don't, will suffer the consequences. Mark 11:23 says that "he shall have whatsoever he saith." What does this really mean? It means exactly what it says! Notice the Bible didn't say, "He shall have whatever he needs," or, "He shall have whatever God has foreordained." You will only have what you say! The word *have* in Greek and English is a verb which means to possess or own. The word *say* (*eipon*) is another verb which means to speak or confess. In other words, you will possess what you confess.

Imagine how many things we have released into our lives by confessing (declaring) the opposite of what God says. For example, "This sickness runs in my family!" or "This pain is killing me!" On the surface these may seem like mere casual expressions, but in reality they are powerful negative confessions. By speaking these words, you are actually giving Satan legal permission to carry out your words in their fullness. Remember this—whatever you speak and believe, you are empowering. If you want to receive healing in your body, speak healing over your body according to God's Word. If you want be free of cancer, speak life instead of death. I cannot tell you how many times I have prayed for people who have, in actuality, negated my prayers with their own negative words. Make sure that you and the people you are praying for understand this profound spiritual principle.

ALIGNING YOUR MOUTH WITH HEAVEN

But what saith it? The word is nigh thee, even in thy mouth, and in thy heart: that is, the word of faith, which we preach (Romans 10:8).

The first step to walking in and manifesting divine healing is aligning your words with heaven. What do I mean by this expression? You must understand that heaven has an agenda as set forth in the Word of God. Heaven's agenda is healing and freedom for God's people. We have to learn to come into agreement with this heavenly reality. How do we do this? We do this by aligning our confession with the Word of God; this is what I call "heavenly alignment."

The beautiful thing about God is that He has already set forth the pattern in His Word for us to follow. We don't have to come up with any original ideas; simply say exactly what He says. Never underestimate the power of heavenly alignment! We said earlier that your mouth is a supernatural orifice or gateway. The Greek word for *mouth* in Romans 10:8 is *stoma*, which means "the edge of the sword." This is quite fascinating! In other words, your mouth is a weapon. Either your words are releasing life, health, and healing, or they are assisting the devil in accomplishing his evil plan; there is no neutral ground.

> *Your mouth is a divine gateway capable of releasing both blessing and curses, good and evil.*

For example, a person facing pain and agony in their physical body may say something like, "This pain is killing me!" or "I can't take this any more; this is horrible!" Let us examine these expressions a bit further. To say that pain is killing you is to confess death, thus giving Satan permission to kill you. Let's define the word *horrible*—causing horror, dreadful, shocking, or ghastly. Is this really what you want? You may be saying to yourself, "It's not that serious!" My friend, you are incorrect—it is that serious! By saying these things passionately and consistently, you are actually aligning your mouth with hell instead of heaven.

Exposing Word Curses

Out of the same mouth proceedeth blessing and cursing. My brethren, these things ought not so to be (James 3:10).

I grew up in a culture and an environment that was filled with negativity. I didn't even realize how negative it was until I became much older. For instance, I would hear people say things like, "You are stupid!" or "That person is an idiot!" Many of you can relate to this. Some of you have said or heard things much more severe, such as, "I hope you die!" "You will never succeed!" or "You will never get married." My friend, these types of statements are not from God. In fact, these are what the Bible calls word curses.

When we think of curses, we often think of a witch with a broomstick or a voodoo priest, but in reality curses can be much more subtle than that. A curse from a biblical standpoint is an imprecation or pronouncement of evil. Any time we speak negative words rooted in fear, hate, bitterness, evil, or destruction, we are in fact releasing curses. What does this have to do with healing? Many sicknesses and physical maladies are rooted in curses. I heard a story one day about a man who was diagnosed with cancer. This man believed God for healing, and he communicated this to his fellow congregants. One day after the church service, a man came up to him and told him that he had a dream, and in this dream he saw the man at his own funeral. To this statement, the man with the cancer immediately rebuked him and said, "I shall live and not die and declare the works of the Lord."

Can you imagine the implications of telling someone that you saw their funeral? This is an example of a curse. Thankfully, the man had enough faith and knowledge to rebuke the person being used by the devil.

> The spoken word sets spiritual forces in motion
> that greatly impact our natural reality.

Oftentimes when I am praying for people dealing with illness, I make it a point to do a thorough inventory of their words. Almost every time, I find that those who are sick have been saying things that contradict the Word of God. For instance, "Pastor Kynan, please pray for me because my life is miserable. Things are getting worse and worse, and I don't know what to do. I feel so depressed and angry. Pray for me!" You may have engaged in this type of negative self-talk before, but make no mistake—this kind of speaking will release destruction into your life. Remember, any language that disempowers you and makes you a victim of your circumstances is satanic.

I am not suggesting that people should lie or exaggerate when it comes to sickness or pain, but I am saying that you must make a habit of only saying what God says. Instead of complaining and speaking death, speak life! "Father, in the midst of this pain, I proclaim that You are the God who heals me. This sickness is not unto death, but I shall live and not die." This is an example of speaking blessing instead of cursing.

CURSING SICKNESS AND DISEASE

And Peter calling to remembrance saith unto him, Master, behold, the fig tree which thou cursedst is withered away (Mark 11:21).

Earlier, we mentioned that the words we speak have a profound effect on our natural reality. This is truer than you can imagine. We also mentioned the importance of speaking blessings over your own life and body according to the Word of God. The inverse is true of sickness and disease. We must learn how to curse sickness and disease in our lives. Remember, your mouth is the divine conduit of blessing *and* curses. We are never to curse people, but we have every right to curse—or pronounce imprecation and judgment—upon sickness and disease. Jesus Himself pronounced a curse over the fig tree in Mark 11. Many people believe that this was a prophetic symbol, but I believe that from a natural standpoint Jesus cursed the fig tree because it was no longer producing fruit. That is to say, the fig tree was not functioning according to the purpose it was given by God.

For many years, I had no concept of this spiritual principle. Now when I minister to the sick, I exercise my spiritual authority in cursing disease, infirmity, sickness, and death. You may be saying to yourself, "I can curse sickness?" Absolutely! In fact, the Bible says:

And he arose out of the synagogue, and entered into Simon's house. And Simon's wife's mother was taken with a great fever; and they besought him for her. And he stood over her, and rebuked the fever; and it left her: and immediately she arose and ministered unto them (Luke 4:38-39).

In Luke's account, Jesus goes into Simon's house and rebukes the fever that was plaguing his mother-in-law. You may have read this passage before and never noticed what I am about to share with you. The word *rebuked* in this passage is the Greek word *epitimaō*, which means "to censure, to adjudge as evil, or to reprove." In other words, Jesus pronounced judgment over the fever and condemned the fever as evil. Simply put, Jesus cursed the fever. Why? This sickness was an evil affliction. If Jesus rebuked fevers and cursed barren trees, then you have every right to do as He did (see John 14:12). I have found this to be especially true of cancers, tumors, and unwanted growths.

HEALING TESTIMONY

There was a lady with a cancerous growth on her face. She asked God to heal her many times and nothing happened. Finally, the Lord spoke to her and told her to speak to that growth and command it to wither and die. This she did for many days. At first, there did not seem to be any change. Like the fig tree in Mark 11, things looked the same. One day, after cursing the growth on her face, she decided to flick it with her finger. To her surprise, the growth fell off her face. Glory to God! Our words are powerful! You can speak to those unwanted growths on your body and command them to dry up by the roots. You can speak to cancer and command it to wither and die, in the name of Jesus. This is very powerful! Don't sit back and tolerate sickness another moment. Tell that infirmity where to go.

When we speak with biblical authority, God synergizes His supernatural power with our words.

Religion and tradition have taught us to simply pray about sickness, but the Word of God is filled with countless examples of Jesus and the disciples rebuking sickness. We too have to talk to the infirmity and command it to go. *This is a proactive approach to healing, as opposed to a passive approach.* Later we will talk about the relationship between healing and deliverance, but we must first understand the responsibility that we have to confess God's Word over ourselves and others.

Years ago, I had severe acne of the skin. At one point, it was so bad that I wore a baseball cap everywhere I went to cover up my forehead. My mother took me to a dermatologist where I was prescribed medication for my skin. The medication worked for a while until the rashes and breakouts would reappear. I did not know what to do! This was a very frustrating time in my life. I thought that it would go away on its own, but it didn't. One day while watching Christian television, the minister said, "If you have acne and you want to be healed, touch the screen." I had never heard of any such thing in my life. I figured I didn't have anything to lose, so I touched the screen and prayed the prayer of faith. There was no immediate transformation, but I began declaring, "My skin is healed and in perfect condition." I cursed the acne by the roots and commanded it to go in Jesus's name. To my amazement, my skin began improving. This happened without the use of prescription drugs or over-the-counter medication. All of a sudden, my skin was perfectly normal. I can't remember the last time I suffered from severe breakouts or anything close to that. This is the power of speaking the blessing over yourself and cursing infirmity in your life.

SUMMARY QUESTIONS

1. What is the biblical definition of confession?

2. What happens when we consistently confess words out of our mouths?

3. What is meant by the term *heavenly alignment?*

4. What is the biblical usage of curses? When and what are we allowed to curse?

CHAPTER 11

HEALING AND DELIVERANCE

And Jesus rebuked the devil; and he departed out of him: and the child was cured from that very hour (Matthew 17:18).

It was commonly understood during the time of Christ that sickness and disease where *primarily* demonic in nature. Although this is not always the case today, many sicknesses can still be attributed to demonic activity. You will often notice Jesus rebuking demonic spirits in the New Testament, and the supernatural healing that ensued. There is a direct correlation between deliverance—people being set free from demonic oppression—and healing.

We said previously that there were three dimensions to healing; these three dimensions are spirit, soul, and body. As we mentioned before, the root cause of all sickness, as we know it, is ultimately spiritual, because of Adam's transgression in the Garden of Eden (see Genesis 3). Therefore, we understand that many diseases today are caused by spiritual forces. In Matthew's account, Jesus rebuked a demonic spirit afflicting a child, and that child was cured immediately. This is amazing! In Luke 10:19, the Bible tells us that we have been given authority over all the power of the devil and nothing shall by any means hurt us. Have you ever considered that the power of the devil includes sickness, disease, infirmity, and even death?

One of the things that really disturbs me is when I hear people make sweeping statements like, "The Lord took my brother in that accident," or, "God caused cancer to kill my sister." This is simply not true according to the Bible! People often attribute tragedy to God when they have no other explanation. We know that God is sovereign and that He knows the time and place of death for every person, but we also know that God is omnibenevolent and that He, through His Son Jesus, came to give us life and not death. John 10:10 tells us:

> The thief cometh not, but for to steal, and to kill, and to destroy: I am come that they might have life, and that they might have it more abundantly.

Being confined to a hospital bed or being bound with chronic sickness does not sound like the abundant life to which Jesus made reference. We must understand that sickness and death were never a part of the original plan of God. The Bible says, "With long life will I satisfy him, and shew him my salvation" (Ps. 91:16). I am by no means suggesting that people who are afflicted by sickness or demonic activity are in some way evil or bad; I am saying that demonic oppression is *never the will of God*. The truth is that there is an inescapable connection between the ministry of healing and the ministry of deliverance. The ministry of deliverance brings about restoration to the spiritual condition of man, thus affecting the soul and body. The Word of God commands us in Mark 16 to "cast out devils." The Bible says:

> And these signs shall follow them that believe; In my name shall they cast out devils; they shall speak with new tongues (Mark 16:17).

DEMONS OF SICKNESS

In my years of ministry, I have come across many situations where people in the body of Christ were being oppressed by demons (demonized). Before I go further, I want to clarify the term *oppression*. When we use the term *oppression,* we are specifically referring to demonic activity in a person's life that keeps them in bondage or prevents them from enjoying the abundant life. For example, addiction is a form of oppression because it restricts a person's ability to function the way God intends. This can be in the form of drugs, alcohol, pornography, gluttony, or self-hatred to name a few. How many people do you know in the body of Christ who are dealing with addictions or depression?

Sickness is another form of oppression because it hinders the operation of the purpose and plan of God in an individual's life. The problem with sickness is that many people fail to acknowledge its demonic nature. Have you ever watched the progression of cancer in a person's life? It is one of the most horrendous things one could ever witness. There is nothing good about cancer; it is completely evil. This is the way God sees all sickness—evil. In fact, I believe that cancer is in itself a demonic manifestation.

The gift of discernment of spirits is useful in identifying the operation of demons of sickness in a person's life.

If we are going to be effective in ministering deliverance to the sick, then we must first understand how to identify demons. What is a demon? How do we identify them? The word *demon* comes from the Greek word *daimonion* (Strong's, G1140), which means "evil spirits or the messengers and ministers of the devil." Simply put, a demon is a fallen angel or disembodied spirit that is evil or malevolent in nature. Demons are responsible for manifesting certain sins, sicknesses, addictions, or other areas of bondage and/or oppression. Sadly, many Christians are ignorant of demons, yet they are very real. Demons are capable of attacking, influencing, and even possessing a human host. This is evident in the case of the Gadarene demoniac (see Mark 5:1-15). It is also important to note that not all sicknesses are demonic. Many diseases originate from diet and lifestyle choices, among other things.

TESTIMONY

When I first became a believer, I experienced a rude awakening when it came to deliverance. One night a friend of mine called and said he wanted to come to my apartment and talk. As you would imagine, I gladly obliged to his request. However, something was very strange. I could hear something very different in his voice. I began to pray in the Spirit. When he arrived, I noticed that his behavior was very unusual, but I continued to speak with him. As we began to talk, he started to manifest a spirit of violence and murder. His face contorted like a lion and he threatened to kill me. He came within three inches of my face and said, "I can really hurt you right now!"

This was definitely not the friend I knew! I immediately responded by saying, "You can't hurt me at all, because I am covered by the blood of the Lamb Jesus. I am not afraid of you. In the name of Jesus, I command you, spirit of murder and death, to come out of him." To my amazement, he was instantly delivered and fell to the ground. Within five minutes he was back to his normal self.

Demons have a mind, will, and emotions and often work to bring people into bondage.

The relationship between demonic activity and sickness is masterfully illustrated in Matthew's gospel account when Jesus healed a boy afflicted by palsy. The Bible records:

> *And when they were come to the multitude, there came to him a certain man, kneeling down to him, and saying, Lord, have mercy on my son: for he is lunatick, and sore vexed: for ofttimes he falleth into the fire, and oft into the water. And I brought him to thy disciples, and they could not cure him. Then Jesus answered and said, O faithless and perverse generation, how long shall I be with you? how long shall I suffer you? bring him hither to me. And Jesus rebuked the devil; and he departed out of him: and the child was cured from that very hour* (Matthew 17:14-18).

It is important to note from the above story that the father refers to his son's condition as *lunatick*. This word comes from the Greek word *selēniazomai* which means "moon-struck" or epilepsy. During ancient biblical times, it was believed that epilepsy was affected by the moon, hence the word *moon-struck*. Simply put, the young boy was having epileptic seizures. Notice that the Bible says, "Jesus rebuked the devil." Why? He discerned that the agency responsible for the boy's seizures was demonic. The moment Jesus cast out the demon of epilepsy, the sickness left immediately. We see that the *spirit of epilepsy* or *lunatick* was throwing the boy into the fire and water. The demonic spirit was imposing its will on the human host in the form of debilitating symptoms and hazardous behavior.

> *Jesus has given us the spiritual authority to cast out devils and cure all manner of diseases.*

In Matthew's account of the epileptic boy, notice that the healing that young man desperately needed was connected to his deliverance from an evil spirit. Before we go further, I want to clarify yet another misconception. I have often heard it debated whether or not a Christian can have a demon. I think every pastor in the world would agree that there are demons operating in the local church, and in many cases these demons operate through people who profess Jesus as Lord. There is a difference between a person being oppressed by a demonic spirit and being possessed by a demonic spirit. Oppression is defined as persecution, maltreatment, or abuse, whereas possession is the state of having, owning, or controlling something.

Based on these simple definitions, it is unreasonable to assume that a born-again, Spirit-filled believer can be demon *possessed* (owned or controlled), but it is evident that there are many Christians who are being demonically *oppressed* (through depression, anxiety, fear, sickness, etc.). I have prayed for, counseled, and ministered to many people who were under satanic oppression. Romans 10:13 tells us, "For whosoever shall call upon the name of the Lord shall be saved." As discussed earlier, the word *saved* is the Greek word *sozo,* which means to be delivered, rescued, or made whole, especially from peril, evil, or danger. You can see then why the Bible says in James 5:15, "And the prayer of faith shall save the sick, and the Lord shall raise him up; and if he have committed sins, they shall be forgiven him."

SICKNESS IS EVIL!

He that committeth sin is of the devil; for the devil sinneth from the beginning. For this purpose the Son of God was manifested, that he might destroy the works of the devil (1 John 3:8).

All throughout Scripture, sickness is depicted as evil, perilous, and hazardous to our well-being. It is never represented as something God uses to teach us a lesson or a seal of piety. People need to be delivered from sickness. Jesus came to destroy the works of the devil. How did He accomplish this task? Acts 10:38 tells us, "How God anointed Jesus of Nazareth with the Holy Ghost and with power: who went about doing good, and healing all that were oppressed of the devil; for God was with him." Jesus destroyed the works of the evil one by healing and delivering all those who were oppressed of the devil. This statement illuminates the truth that sickness is in fact oppression, and *all* oppression is satanic.

The reason this is so important to know is people will no longer easily accept sickness when they know it is from the devil. The biggest deception in the church today is the belief that sickness is from God. If a person believes that sickness is from the Lord, they will gladly embrace it. The reality is that sickness, in all forms it manifests, is designed to bring people under the oppression of the evil one. Does God want His people oppressed by the devil? Absolutely not! In fact, did you know that there are certain sicknesses attached to certain sins and demonic spirits? Earlier, we mentioned the importance of understanding the New Testament definition of salvation as deliverance from evil or peril. It is possible for people to be saved in their spirit man and still bound with demonic activity in their soul. This is the case with many in the church today. They are saved and often love God, but they are still bound with demons of sickness and disease. Many of these illnesses are nothing more than demonic manifestations. Below is a list of different categories of sickness that we have found to be associated with demonic activity.

Sexual Immorality

We have found that certain chronic conditions can be attached to demons of lust, adultery, pornography, and sexual immorality. For instance, prostate cancer, cervical cancer, ovarian cancer, lupus, HIV/AIDS, multiple sclerosis, ovarian cysts, and thyroid disorders.

Hatred, Strife, and Offense

Many people are unknowingly opening the door to sickness and disease through bitterness, hatred, and a refusal to forgive. Demons of sickness can enter into the body through hurt and offense. Such demonic manifestations are breast cancer, dementia, Alzheimer's, brain tumors, stomach cancer, leukemia, bone marrow cancer, osteoarthritis, rheumatoid arthritis, gout, acne, dermatitis, male and female pattern baldness, muscular dystrophy, and Crohn's disease.

Witchcraft, Sorcery, and Control

We have had extensive experience in ministering to people who have been under the influence of or practicing witchcraft, or have a spirit of witchcraft operating in their family or church community. Many diseases are immediately healed when the demons of manipulation, control, and sorcery are cast out. Such conditions are miscarriages, sterility, barrenness, chronic vaginal bleeding, diabetes, depression, ADHD, migraine headaches, autism, malignant tumors, multiple personality disorder, bipolar disorder, schizophrenia, dyslexia, detached retina, and cataracts.

To clarify, I am not suggesting that if you are experiencing these illnesses it is because you have sinned in some way, but I am saying that deliverance from these spirits has brought about divine healing in many people's lives. This is by no means an exhaustive list.

HOW DEMONS ENTER

When the unclean spirit is gone out of a man, he walketh through dry places, seeking rest, and findeth none. Then he saith, I will return into my house from whence I came out; and when he is come, he findeth it empty, swept, and garnished. Then goeth he, and taketh with himself seven other spirits more wicked than himself, and they enter in and dwell there: and the last state of that man is worse than the first. Even so shall it be also unto this wicked generation (Matthew 12:43-45).

Remember, we stated that demons are disembodied spirits which have the ability to take residence in the body and soul of a person—a human host. These spirits can cause physical sickness, mental illness, emotional turmoil, and spiritual bondage. The blood of the lamb covers those of us who are born again, but Christians can still be demonized through the gateway of the soul—the mind, will, and emotions. The Bible tells us in Third John 1:2, "Beloved, I wish above all things that thou mayest prosper and be in health, even as thy soul prospereth." Notice that the Bible says that we are able to prosper (*euodoo*, Strong's, G2137) and be in health as our soul prospers. That is to say, our soul is a gateway through which we manifest the abundant life, including healing. The soul can also be an entrance for demonic activity, including sickness and disease. There are four ways that demons can enter:

1. Our thought life

2. Our words

3. Through sin, including our sins and the sins of others

4. Points of contact

THE GATEWAY OF THE MIND

The Bible says in Proverbs 23:7, "For as he thinketh in his heart, so is he." In other words, what you set your mind on you will ultimately manifest. Our thought life is very powerful because everything we do or say begins with a thought. When people harbor thoughts of offense, bitterness, hatred, lust, or fear, it can open the door to demonic oppression. The Bible tells us in Second Corinthians 10:5, "Casting down imaginations, and every high thing that exalteth itself against the knowledge of God, and bringing into captivity every thought to the obedience of Christ."

Satan often attacks people in the area of their thoughts. What are you meditating on consistently? For example, a person finds a growth on their leg, and the first thought that comes to them is *cancer*. If the person continues to meditate on that thought, it will open the door to a spirit of fear and ultimately bring about lying symptoms in their body. We must take our thoughts captive in order to walk in true freedom and healing.

THE GATEWAY OF THE MOUTH

Our words have a profound effect on our lives and the lives of others. The Bible says, "Death and life are in the power of the tongue: and they that love it shall eat the fruit thereof" (Prov. 18:21). What we say can bring life or death! This is a spiritual reality. When we speak words that are contrary to the will of God, we are in reality inviting demonic activity to manifest. For example, a lying symptom comes to a person's body, and instead of casting down the evil imagination, they embrace it as real and begin to say things like, "I am so sick!" Those fear-filled words give legal right to the enemy to manifest demons of sickness and oppression in their physical body. We counter this demonic activity by speaking faith-filled words according to the will of God. The Bible says, "But what saith it? The word is nigh thee, even in thy mouth, and in thy heart: that is, the word of faith, which we preach" (Rom. 10:8). The Word of God in your mouth can bring healing and deliverance to your mind, body, and soul.

THE GATEWAY OF SIN

Jesus answered them, Verily, verily, I say unto you, Whosoever committeth sin is the servant of sin (John 8:34).

One of the most fundamental ways demonic activity enters a believer's life is through willful and unrepentant sin. Jesus said that he that commits sin is the servant of sin. There are two Greek words we need to examine in order to understand this passage properly. The first word is the word *commit*. This comes from the Greek word *poieō*, which means "to make, produce, or construct." In other words, it means "to practice" sin. To practice sin means to continually violate God's Word in a particular area of your life. For instance, God tells us in the Word to abstain from sexual immorality. Practicing sexual sin can lead to a person being demonized. Remember, our bodies are the temple of God. If we engage in willful sin with our temple, we are opening the door to the enemy to oppress our physical bodies. (This does not mean that if you sin you deserve to be sick.)

The other word we must examine is the word *servant*. This comes from the Greek word *doulos*, which means "slave, bondservant, or one who surrenders their will to another." If we continually practice rebellion against God's Word by engaging in willful sin, we are inviting sin to dominate our lives. Sin is the environment in which the devil has a legal right to operate. Many people are experiencing chronic sickness in their bodies because they are harboring bitterness and resentment in their hearts willfully. This resentment is fertile ground for demonic activity, including sickness, oppression, and disease. We close the door to the enemy by confessing our sins before God and turning from willful sin through genuine repentance. Also, sin produces shame and condemnation. If a person is operating in guilt or shame, they will find it difficult to exercise their faith and confidence to receive healing and deliverance.

POINTS OF CONTACT

Another way that demons can enter a person's life is through "points of contact." A point of contact can be any person, object, or activity through which the enemy gains access to our lives. This can include practicing or entertaining witchcraft, purchasing ancient artifacts, or watching certain movies or television programs. To give you an example of points of contact, one night I decided to watch a horror movie while my children were asleep. While I was watching the movie, I noticed that my children were restless and coughing. The next morning, they reported to us that they had terrible dreams that night. I unknowingly opened the door to the enemy through the portal of my television. Another example is artifacts that we may purchase from yard sales or receive from a friend. One time the Lord told me that a certain painting in my home of a Haitian village had a spirit of lust attached to it. Once I destroyed the painting, I noticed that the atmosphere of our home drastically changed for the better. Ask the Holy Spirit to reveal to you any points of contact in your life that have given the enemy access to your health or freedom.

> *Many areas of sickness are instantly healed when the door through which that sickness entered is closed.*

As one who will minister healing to others, it is very important to exercise authority over various demonic spirits that may be causing sickness and infirmity to operate in an individual's life. The Lord will give you discernment to know whether or not a sickness is demonically inspired. The Lord will also give you words of knowledge to call out specific infirmities when praying for the sick. As you develop a sensitivity to the Spirit, you will become more and more effective in healing the sick.

HEALING AND DELIVERANCE PRAYER

Father, in the name of Jesus Christ, I come to You now as my Deliverer and Redeemer. I ask you to forgive me of all my sins, known and unknown. I repent of all sins operating in my life. Right now, I expose my entire spirit, soul, and body to the Word of God, the blood of Jesus, and the Fire of the Holy Spirit; I command anything operating in my life that was not planted by You to be uprooted. From this day forward, I command all spirits of sickness, disease, bondage, and infirmity to cease operations in my soul and body in Jesus's name. I declare that I am 100 percent healed and delivered in Jesus's name. Amen!

SUMMARY QUESTIONS

1. What are demons? How do they influence sickness and disease?

2. Can a Christian have a demon?

3. How do demons enter a person's life?

CHAPTER 12

BREAKING BARRIERS TO HEALING

And he could there do no mighty work, save that he laid his hands upon a few sick folk, and healed them (Mark 6:5).

What prevents people from receiving their healing? I have asked this question many times throughout my life as a believer, and I am sure that you have asked this question as well. We have seen people die from sickness prematurely, and we have watched others suffer the agony of a debilitating sickness for several years, some never receiving their miracle. The more I pray for people to be healed, the more my eyes are opened to the common barriers that prevent many well-meaning believers from receiving their healing.

When I was growing up in church, I often heard the expression, "The Lord must be teaching me something through this!" The irony of this statement was that

I couldn't find that concept anywhere in the Bible. I later discovered the reason why I couldn't find that particular statement in the Bible was because it's not biblical. The Scripture affirms that it is the perfect will of God for people to be healed. If this statement is true, then why don't people get healed? There are several reasons, based on the Bible, why people don't get healed. I will share them with you in just a moment, but before I do that I want to take a moment to encourage you. You may have a loved one who is battling cancer or some other "terminal" or "chronic" illness, or you may be fighting sickness yourself. Regardless of what the situation may be, you must resolve this truth in your spirit: "*God wants you healed!*"

In this chapter we will explore the ten common barriers to healing. This is by no means an exhaustive list, but a powerful guide that will help you to identify and break barriers to receiving the miracle of healing.

1. LACK OF KNOWLEDGE

My people are destroyed for lack of knowledge: because thou hast rejected knowledge, I will also reject thee, that thou shalt be no priest to me: seeing thou hast forgotten the law of thy God, I will also forget thy children (Hosea 4:6).

One of the most common reasons people are unable to receive their healing is a lack of knowledge. What do we mean when we use the expression *lack of knowledge*? Hosea says, "My people are destroyed for lack of knowledge"; this is the

Hebrew word *da'ath* (Strong's, H1847), which means "lack of perception, discernment, or understanding." When you look at it from this perspective you can clearly see that the Bible is telling us that a lack of discernment can negatively impact our lives. In fact, the Hebrew word used for "destroyed" is the word *damah* (Strong's, H1820), which means "to be cut off."

I have often heard the expression, "What you don't know won't hurt you!" or "Ignorance is bliss!" Nothing could be further from the truth! Again, when the Bible uses the expression *lack of knowledge* it is referring specifically to a lack of discernment concerning God's will. Many people are being "cut off" from the covenant promise of healing because they are ignorant (lack discernment) of what the Word of God says. I cannot tell you the countless times I have attempted to minister healing to someone only for their lack of knowledge to stand as a barrier between them and their breakthrough.

The Bible doesn't just say that people are cut off for a lack of knowledge, but Hosea 4:6 also says, "Because thou hast rejected knowledge." It is not simply that people are unaware or undiscerning, but there is an element of stubbornness that must be addressed. Many people are in essence rejecting their own healing and deliverance. The solution to this dilemma is receiving revelation from God's Word. Revelation brings change!

2. DOUBT AND UNBELIEF

Seeing therefore it remaineth that some must enter therein, and they to whom it was first preached entered not in because of unbelief (Hebrews 4:6).

The simple reality is that everything that God has promised in His Word, including healing, can only be received by faith. Doubt and unbelief create a barrier that prevents people from consistently receiving their healing. Even in the earthly ministry of Jesus, many were not able to experience the fullness of God's will to heal them due to doubt and unbelief.

Many people find the issue of faith very personal and private, and they are extremely offended if it is ever implied that they do not believe. Let us take a moment to define unbelief. The Greek word for "unbelief" in this passage is *apeitheia* (Strong's, G543), which means "obstinacy, obstinate opposition to the divine will." It is where we get the English word *apathy*. To operate in unbelief is to be obstinate, resistant, or apathetic toward the Word of God. In other words, unbelief is a system of thinking and behaving that opposes or contradicts God's will. For instance, many people say that they believe God to heal them, but their actions contradict that claim. They spend countless hours telling people how sick they are and how horrible their condition is. This is the definition of doubt and unbelief.

The Bible says that the children of Israel did not enter into the Promised Land because of unbelief. They didn't act on the Word of God. Faith is the revelation of God's Word in action. To believe is to act on the truth of God's Word. Whenever we act on God's Word, we are affirming His Word to be true and we are posturing ourselves to receive the full manifestation of what we believe. There are instances in the Bible where people were healed even though they didn't have the faith to receive. These circumstances were much more rare and would be actually categorized as miracles. It is definitely true that God does many things in our lives as an act of His grace and compassion, but when it comes to consistently receiving and maintaining our healing, faith is absolutely necessary.

3. FALSE TEACHING

For the time will come when they will not endure sound doctrine; but after their own lusts shall they heap to themselves teachers, having itching ears; and they shall turn away their ears from the truth, and shall be turned unto fables (2 Timothy 4:3-4).

The kind and quality of teaching that we are exposed to has a profound impact on our ability to receive and walk in divine healing. In fact, the Bible says in Romans 10:14, "How then shall they call on him in whom they have not believed? and how shall they believe in him of whom they have not heard? and how shall they hear without a preacher?" Our ability to place a demand on God's character and nature is directly dependent on our knowledge of who He is, and that knowledge comes from sound teaching. If you are being taught that God wants you sick, then you will not be able to extend your faith beyond that doctrine. Remember this—right teaching produces right thinking, and right thinking produces right believing. Ultimately, what we believe and how we believe will determine what we receive.

I can recall a conversation I had with a man in a bookstore who told me that Jesus doesn't heal today. This belief is commonly known as cessationism. The problem with this belief is that it is unbiblical. When a person holds to an erroneous belief such as cessationism, they will not be able to manifest the power of God to deal with sickness and disease in their lives; the barrier of false teaching blocks them. We must make sure that the beliefs that we hold about God are foremost rooted in Scripture, and we must make sure that we are rightly dividing God's Word for ourselves; your healing depends on it!

4. PRIDE

Pride goeth before destruction, and an haughty spirit before a fall (Proverbs 16:18).

Oftentimes, people are unable to embrace healing because of pride. What is pride? When we use the term *pride*, what we are referring to is a vain concentration on self. This is the opposite of humility. One day I was in the Christian bookstore, and there was a man with whom I spoke about divine healing. Before I could even fully express my point, the gentleman stated (in a very aggressive tone), "Yeah, I know about healing! If God decides to heal a person, He will." This was a very disappointing conversation, because the man was full of pride. He assumed that he knew things that he really did not know.

The Bible says that pride comes before destruction. That is to say, pride is the prerequisite for destruction. The word *destruction* is the Hebrew word *sheber*, which means "breach, fracture, crush, or break." The enemy, due to pride, is breaching many people. On the other hand, humility postures us to receive from God, but pride causes us to resist the very miracle that we need. Too many people in the body of Christ are operating in religious pride. They refuse to humble themselves and admit that they don't know and that they need help.

On another occasion, I offered to pray for a person who was dealing with a severe illness and they said, "No!" Apparently, the notion of praying for them was offensive to them. They were tired of people always asking to pray and treating them as if they were victims. Though I can understand the frustration of feeling patronized, we must be careful not to operate in fleshly pride that can undermine the very breakthrough that we need. I never turn down prayer, so long as the person praying for me is sincere and operating in the right spirit.

5. SPIRITUAL BLINDNESS

*In whom the god of this world hath **blinded the minds** of them which believe not, lest the light of the glorious gospel of Christ, who is the image of God, should shine unto them* (2 Corinthians 4:4).

There are so many people in the body of Christ who are walking in spiritual blindness. What do we mean by "spiritual blindness"? The Bible says in Second Corinthians that the god of this world has blinded the minds of those who do not believe. The word *blinded* comes from the Greek word *typhloō*, which means "to blunt mental discernment or to darken the mind." In essence, spiritual blindness is the condition of being desensitized or "darkened" to the things of God, especially healing and miracles.

Recently, there was a conference held by a prominent Christian pastor in America who took upon himself the daunting task of proving that the gifts of the Spirit are no longer in operation and that miracles (such as healing the sick, raising the dead, and cleansing the leper) no longer happen today. This pastor put together this conference with the sole purpose of discrediting modern-day miracles and the ministers who claim to perform them. This really grieved my spirit, because the Bible clearly says that Jesus is the same yesterday, today, and forever (see Heb. 13:8). The Bible also says, "Verily, verily, I say unto you, He that believeth on me, the works that I do shall he do also; and greater works than these shall he do; because I go unto my Father" (John 14:12).

Now, I can show you the grammatical and contextual framework to prove that Jesus meant exactly what He said, but it would suffice to say that anyone able to read the Bible should know that this is true. What then is the problem? Satan has blinded the minds of people (such as this minister and others) through doubt, unbelief, and skepticism. The enemy has convinced them that healing is evil rather than good. The moment a person embraces a lie, a spirit of deception enters in that has the power to prevent them from receiving from God. The devil wants the church to reject their healing. Beloved, give him no place!

6. FEAR

For God hath not given us the spirit of fear; but of power, and of love, and of a sound mind (2 Timothy 1:7).

Another insidious factor that can hinder a person from receiving their healing is fear. What is fear? In the book of Second Timothy, the Bible says that God has not given us a spirit of fear. This is the Greek word *deilia*, which means "timidity, fearfulness, and cowardice." We cannot receive (embrace) our healing if we are operating in timidity or cowardice. Walking in healing and deliverance requires boldness and power. Another way to describe fear is *false evidence appearing real* (F.E.A.R.). The enemy attempts to manipulate people through their five senses, to convince them that the promise of their healing will never come into manifestation; this is a lie! Whether it is the thought that tells a person that their cancer will return or the suggestion that a certain disease is incurable, it is all a manifestation of fear.

We cannot operate in fear and faith at the same time. We must make a choice. God has not given us a spirit of fear, which means that fear is a spirit, and this spirit comes from the evil one. Instead, He has given us the spirit of power, love, and soundness of mind. This power (*dynamis*) is the explosive, miracle-working power of God. Because fear is both a spiritual force and a belief system, we rid ourselves of fear by meditating on the Word of God and embracing His unconditional love. God's Word changes our belief system, and His love drives out fear (see 1 John 4:18). Fear is simply *false evidence appearing real*. You must make up in your mind that the evidence of God's Word is the *only* evidence that you will believe.

7. ANGER TOWARD GOD

Be not hasty in thy spirit to be angry: for anger resteth in the bosom of fools (Ecclesiastes 7:9).

You cannot receive from someone you are angry with. If a person is angry with God because they believe that He is the one afflicting them with sickness, then they will find it extremely difficult to embrace their healing. I have seen this manifest in many situations. Once, I encountered a young lady who was angry with God for "allowing" an accident that caused her body physical damage. This anger toward God prevented her from receiving what God was so graciously willing to give her. She often made statements like, "Why are other people getting healed and not me?" This kind of thinking is counterproductive and even damaging to a person's faith.

If you are serious about healing, you must break the barrier of anger and frustration and make the decision that your healing is more important than being angry with God over what you believe He has allowed in your life. Guard your heart against any thoughts or feelings that would cause you to assume the posture of a victim.

8. Unforgiveness

Therefore I say unto you, What things soever ye desire, when ye pray, believe that ye receive them, and ye shall have them. And when ye stand praying, forgive, if ye have ought against any: that your Father also which is in heaven may forgive you your trespasses (Mark 11:24-25).

There is an inseparable relationship between healing and forgiveness. In fact, there is a healing dimension to forgiveness. The Bible says that when we stand praying, we ought to forgive. If we do not forgive those who trespass against us, then God won't forgive us. For many, this is a very problematic biblical truth. First of all, what does it mean to forgive? The word *forgive* comes from the Greek word *aphiēmi*, which means "to send away or to release." Simply put, forgiveness is the act of releasing offenses, trespasses, hurts, and debts.

What does this have to do with healing? Though God has judicially pardoned us in Christ, He still holds us accountable to walk in forgiveness in our earthly relationships. Refusing to forgive creates a prison of torment and gives demons access to our heart, mind, and physical health. Furthermore, a refusal to forgive will inhibit a person's faith from working the way it should. Remember, faith works by love (see Gal. 5:6). We cannot receive healing without faith. I have witnessed so many people being afflicted in their bodies because they refused to release people who wounded them. I have also seen countless others receive their breakthrough the very moment they decided to forgive their offender.

9. Demonic Strongholds

And, behold, there was a woman which had a spirit of infirmity eighteen years, and was bowed together, and could in no wise lift up herself (Luke 13:11).

There are many physical and mental illnesses that are directly caused by demons. There are also many people who are unable to receive their healing because they do not recognize that they are under demonic oppression. Once, I ministered to a man who was bound with a chronic illness; the moment I saw him in the hospital, I discerned that the spirit of death was oppressing him. When I rebuked the spirit of death attempting to take his life, he immediately began to recover.

There are many sicknesses that are 100 percent demonic in nature. Jesus encountered a woman who had what He identified as a spirit of infirmity. This comes from the Greek word *astheneia*, which means "want of strength, weakness, and feebleness." This spirit of infirmity became a barrier between her and the manifestation of her healing. There are many people who have been battling chronic, prolonged conditions because of this same spirit. Fortunately, Jesus discerned the spiritual forces behind her physical condition. Ask God to grant you discerning of spirits so that you can recognize the nature and source of each illness you encounter. Once a spirit of infirmity is broken, healing will more easily manifest.

10. Carnal Mind

Because the carnal mind is enmity against God: for it is not subject to the law of God, neither indeed can be (Romans 8:7).

The Bible says that the carnal mind is enmity against God. What does this mean? This means that the carnal mind is the enemy of God, because the carnal mind is alien to spiritual things. Remember, healing is first and foremost a spiritual reality. What do we mean when we say *carnal mind*? The carnal mind refers to the sensuous nature of man; in other words, the carnal mind focuses on the gratification of the five natural senses (sight, touch, taste, feeling, etc.).

Many people are unable to receive their healing because they are operating in a carnal mentality. For instance, God tells them through His Word that they are healed, and because they don't see the healing manifest right away they assume that the word is not true. The carnal mind only focus on the natural reality of things but rejects the higher spiritual truth. We overcome the carnal mind by taking ungodly thoughts captive according to Second Corinthians 10:5. We must cast down wicked imaginations and every logic or excuse hostile to God's Word. Once we do this, we will be able to accept the truth of God's Word and act on it accordingly.

SUMMARY QUESTIONS

1. What are the ten barriers to healing listed in the Bible?

2. What is the most common barrier to healing and how does one overcome it?

3. How does a lack of knowledge prevent people from receiving their healing?

4. How do we overcome the carnal mind?

CHAPTER 13

FAITH AND HEALING

*But Jesus turned him about, and when he saw her, he said, Daughter, be of good comfort; thy **faith** hath made thee whole. And the woman was made whole from that hour* (Matthew 9:22).

A s you probably realize by now, faith is the key to receiving your healing and walking in God's miraculous power. Everything in the Kingdom of God revolves around faith in God's Word. The Bible says, "Now faith is the substance of things hoped for, the evidence of things not seen. ...But without faith it is impossible to please him: for he that cometh to God must believe that he is, and that he is a rewarder of them that diligently seek him" (Heb. 11:1,6). It is clear from Scripture that faith is paramount to our Christian experience. The Bible refers to faith as the "substance"; this comes from the Greek word *hypostasis*, which means "substructure, foundation, or support." So we see that faith is the foundation of everything that we are able to receive from God.

Hebrews 11:6 goes further to say that without faith it is impossible to please God. Did you realize that it is impossible to please God without faith? Countless people around the world have no understanding of what real biblical faith is all about. Why do I make such a bold statement? The reason is very simple! Throughout my ministry as a pastor and teacher, I have witnessed people become frustrated, disappointed, and even angry with God because they lacked a biblical understanding of faith. Simply put, faith is our conviction and trust in the Word of God.

Faith is the revelation of God's Kingdom in the now! It is the confidence that what God has spoken is a sure foundation.

The Bible says in Matthew 9:22 that the woman with an issue of blood was made whole by her faith. In the Amplified Bible it says, "Your faith has made you well." I want us to take a moment and think about the implications of that statement. If our faith has the power to make us well, then we must walk by faith in order to receive the blessing of health that God has ordained for our lives. Faith is the divine catalyst that releases the power of supernatural healing. How do we obtain faith? The Bible says in Romans 10:17, "So then faith cometh by hearing, and hearing by the word of God." The word *hearing* is the Greek word *akoē*, which means "sense of hearing." The Bible goes further to say that "hearing" (*akoē*) comes by the Word of God.

When the Bible refers to the Word, it is not just talking about the written Word of God, but it is talking about the *rhēma* or the living and revealed Word of God. Simply put, faith comes to us through the revelation of God's Word. The more we receive revelation, the more we are able to release our faith for divine healing. The beauty of this is that we already have faith, because the Word of God lives on the inside of us. Jesus is the living Word, and if you have received Jesus, then you have also received His supernatural faith. The key is revelation. Revelation brings manifestation! The more you meditate on the Word of God, the stronger your faith will become.

FAITH IN THE NOW

Oftentimes, when people think of faith they think of something that they expect to happen in the future. You have probably heard people say things such as, "I know God is going to heal me one day!" Unfortunately, I have heard people make this statement all the way to the grave. Why? Our faith and our healing are a present reality. Faith is not futuristic in nature, but faith exists in the *now!* What do I mean by the expression "Faith exists in the now"? In Acts 9:34, the Bible records: "And Peter said unto him, Aeneas,

Jesus Christ maketh thee whole: arise, and make thy bed. And he arose *immediately*."

Many of us have read this Scripture, but there is an aspect to this verse that many people tend to neglect. Noticed that when Peter said, "Jesus Christ maketh the whole: arise and make thy bed," the next statement says, "And he arose immediately." Why is this so important to highlight? The word *immediately* comes from the Greek word *eutheōs,* which means "straightway or forthwith." So we see that Aeneas (the crippled man) acted on God's Word instantly, without hesitation. He did not relegate his miracle to some future time, but he had a revelation in his inner being that God's Word was true *here and now.*

> *The moment we receive revelation from the Word of God, we are empowered to step into the fullness of what God has promised.*

The revelation that faith is in the now and not in the future has been one of the most powerful truths that I have come to understand in my spiritual life. This truth has radically reshaped my paradigm and changed the way I approach healing forever. Whether you are believing God for your own healing or preparing to minister healing to others, it is important to know how biblical faith operates. God is not going to heal anyone! Why?

Healing is a finished work. The only thing left to do is receive it and walk in it by faith. That means that when you pray for someone who has been afflicted by sickness and disease, you must believe that they have already received their miracle "immediately" in that moment. Stop saying, "God is going to heal that person," or, "God is going to heal me!" Faith says, "I am already healed by the stripes of the Lord Jesus and I receive my healing *now!*"

So many people are suffering needlessly because they postpone their faith and healing to the future, rather than embrace it in the present. Jesus is the Healer today! His power is available to heal and restore right now! All we have to do is confidently receive what He has made available to us in His Word. No more waiting periods. What would happen if every believer in the body of Christ embraced the truth that faith is in the now? What would take place if every person who prayed for the sick believed in their heart that healing was a finished work? I believe that we would see a widespread manifestation of the healing power of God. Hospitals would empty out and millions of people would begin walking in divine health. It is time for us to take God at His Word and stop making excuses. Faith is revelation and revelation is the supernatural key to manifestation.

FAITH IS THE SUBSTANCE

Earlier, we brought out the fact that faith is the substance of things hoped for and the evidence of things not seen (see Heb. 11:1). I believe that it is extremely important for us to explore this concept further. We stated previously that the word *substance* means "support" or "substructure." This means that faith is the foundation of our spiritual lives. Like any natural building, the strength of the foundation will determine the integrity of the entire structure. Without a strong foundation, a building is bound to collapse.

This is exactly what is happening in the church today. Millions of people are experiencing a "spiritual collapse" because of a wrong understanding of real faith. Many people believe that faith is a feeling. So when they "feel" God's presence or their circumstances are favorable, they trust God, but when they endure adverse situations, their faith wavers. This is not faith at all. In fact, people who engage in this practice are what I call "fair-weather Christians." When everything goes well, they praise God, but when things are difficult, they become despondent and angry with God. Jesus said, "Therefore whosoever heareth these sayings of mine, and doeth them, I will liken him unto a wise man, which built his house upon a rock" (Matt. 7:24).

As you can see from the text, our faith is a response to the Word of God. The way we respond to what God says will determine our success or failure. Those who hear God's words and act on them are establishing their spiritual house on a rock. The hearing that Jesus mentions is not simply a natural hearing, but it comes from the Greek word *akouō*, which means "to be endowed with the faculty of hearing, not deaf." In other words, there is a spiritual hearing necessary to walk in real Bible faith.

> *Our ability to hear and act on the Word of God will determine the strength of our foundation.*

Simply put, faith is a right response to the Word of God based on revelation. Jesus stated in Matthew 7:26 that those who hear His words and don't do them are like those who built their houses on sand. Can you imagine a house being built on sand? There is only one inevitable outcome to such a scenario—utter destruction and catastrophic damage. This is why it is critical for us to meditate upon God's Word continually. The more we hear the Word, the more faith will rise up in our spirit.

The other component is doing what the Word says. IWe must act on the Word of God in order to see transformation in our lives. Faith is the revelation of God's Word in action; therefore, we must be doers of the Word and not just hearers. Are you a doer of the Word? When you see a sick person, do you pray for them according to Mark 16? This is the key to releasing God's supernatural power in your life and the lives of those around you. The Bible says that faith without works is dead (see James 2:26). This simply means that faith without corresponding action is lifeless. We must act on what we believe! I challenge you today to take action based on the Word of God. Whatever He says, do it!

HEALING PRAYER

Father, in the name of Jesus Christ I thank You for who You are and all that You have done. In accordance with Your Word, I declare that I possess great faith. Faith is the substance of things hoped for and the evidence of things not seen; therefore, I release my faith to receive the unseen reality of healing. I trust Your Word as the final authority in my life and stand upon it to receive the promise of healing and deliverance in my life and the lives of those for whom I pray. Faith is the revelation of God's Word in action; therefore, I am a doer of the Word of God and not a hearer only. I acknowledge by faith that I am fully equipped and thoroughly furnished to minister divine healing to the sick in Jesus's name. Amen!

SUMMARY QUESTIONS

1. What is the biblical definition of faith?

2. What is the relationship between faith and healing?

3. What does the Bible mean when it says, "Faith comes by hearing, and hearing by the Word"?

4. What do we mean when we say faith operates in the *now opposed to the future?*

CHAPTER 14

HEALING MYTHS

But refuse and avoid irreverent legends (profane and impure and godless fictions, mere grandmothers' tales) and silly myths, and express your disapproval of them. Train yourself toward godliness (piety), [keeping yourself spiritually fit] (1 Timothy 4:7 AMP).

The Word of God gives us a very strong admonition to avoid myths and fables. The same holds true as it relates to the subject of healing. Unfortunately, there are many myths about healing that have been propagated in the church by religious leaders. Like all myths, these fables seem harmless until you make the mistake of actually believing them. For example, many people hold to the popular myth that God uses sickness to teach us a lesson. You have probably heard this expression at some point in your life, whether directly or indirectly. Nothing could be further from the truth. In Acts 10:38, the Word of God says, "How God anointed Jesus of Nazareth with the Holy Ghost and with power: who went about doing good, and healing all that were oppressed of the devil; for God was with him." Jesus, who is the express image of the Father, went about healing *all* who were sick.

This doesn't look like God using sickness to teach people a lesson to me. If God were in the business of using sickness to teach people a lesson, then He must not have been a very good businessman, because He would have been undermining His own business through His Son Jesus. The truth is that God was never in the business of sickness and disease and never will be. Remember, any belief that disempowers us is not from God. The Word of God says in Luke 10:19, "Behold, I give unto you power to tread on serpents and scorpions, and over all the power of the enemy: and nothing shall by any means hurt you."

> God will never use something that is contrary to His nature to instruct us, and sickness is contrary to God's nature.

Jesus said in Matthew 7:11, "If *ye* then, *being evil*, know how to give good gifts unto your children, how much more shall your Father which is in heaven give good things to them that ask him?" What did Jesus mean by this expression? Man is finite and flawed in his sinful unregenerate state, yet the most carnal among us would not even fathom purposely doing something that would jeopardize our children's well-being. Would you throw your child in a tank full of sharks to teach them not to use profanity or to abstain from sex before marriage? Would you bathe your child in acid to teach them to obey you? God forbid! Why then would we assume that God would use cancer to teach one of His children?

The only lesson that I ever learned from sickness is that I don't ever want to be sick again. The truth is that God is omnibenevolent, which simply means that He is always good. As the saying goes, "God is good, all the time, and all the time, God is good!" I am not suggesting that God doesn't discipline us. It is clear from Scripture that God corrects His children, but He does not and will not use sickness to do it. God corrects His children through His Word and the supernatural work of the Holy Spirit in our hearts. If you get your theology on God's nature right, you will get your theology on healing right every time!

HEALING IS NOT AVAILABLE TODAY

One of the most disturbing myths I have heard about healing is the myth (as it relates to healing) that God is not the same God today that He was during the time the Bible was written. This myth suggests that God doesn't perform healing miracles anymore. I have heard countless arguments about the assumption that healing gifts are not in operation today. There was even a conversation I had with someone at a Christian bookstore about their difficulty believing in healing. He said to me that he was very skeptical of "stuff like that." Ironically, "stuff like that" was the foundation of the early church as well as Jesus's ministry on earth.

> *Jesus Christ is the same yesterday, today, and forever, which means that He is still the healer.*

I want to refer to a Scripture in Luke 4: "The spirit of the Lord is upon me, because he hath anointed me to preach the gospel to the poor; he hath sent me to heal the broken-hearted, to preach deliverance to captives, and recovering of sight to the blind, to set at liberty them that are bruised, to preach the acceptable year of the Lord" (Luke 4:18-19). We see in this passage of Scripture that Jesus was sent by God to do all the aforementioned things. One of those things is to heal the brokenhearted. The word used for *heal* in this particular verse is the Greek work *omai*, translated "to cure, heal, make whole."

To suggest that Jesus no longer heals today is to suggest that He is not the same Jesus that the Bible demonstrates, which is also to suggest that the Word of God is fallible. I choose to believe that God is the same God He was in the beginning of creation and that His Word remains true. The reason the devil propagates this insidious myth is because He wants the church to subconsciously embrace a powerless Jesus. There is only one real Jesus, and He is full of power and authority. The devil knows that if people embrace God's plan to heal the sick (as revealed in the ministry of

Christ), they will dismantle the kingdom of darkness, sickness by sickness.

The truth is that we have been given authority by God to cure all manner of sicknesses and diseases, and we are no longer victims of the devil. The curse of sin, death, poverty, and sickness has been broken once and for all. We no longer have to live under the oppressive hand of the evil one. Don't you find it ironic that people believe that the power of God is no longer available, but no one questions whether the devil has stopped being the devil? We see evil all over the world today displayed in various forms, but I have never heard any reasonable preacher suggest that the devil doesn't exist or that evil is no longer operating today. The devil is alive and well, and the Lord Jesus is even more alive and well. He is still healing the sick and raising the dead. He is still Jehovah Rapha! All we have to do is receive His healing power by faith.

CHAPTER 15

SIGNS, WONDERS, AND MIRACLES

Ye men of Israel, hear these words; Jesus of Nazareth, a man approved of God among you by miracles and wonders and signs, which God did by him in the midst of you, as ye yourselves also know. (Acts 2:22)

Whether you realize it or not, signs, wonders, and miracles should be a normal part of the Christian life. The Bible tells us in John 14:12, "Verily, verily, I say unto you, He that believeth on me, the works that I do shall he do also; and greater works than these shall he do; because I go unto my Father." Can you imagine this? Can you believe that Jesus has invited every believer to do the same things that He did and greater? Well, He did! Most people don't believe this, and that is the very reason why they don't experience miracles in their daily lives. For many years, I couldn't believe this truth either! Even though I was a part of a church that preached about the power of God, I rarely saw any miracles take place. Miracles are the dinner bell of the gospel; they point people to the power and love of God and the need for salvation.

What is the Bible referring to when it talks about signs, wonders, and miracles? I am glad you asked! First let us define what a sign is; the word *sign* comes from the Greek word *sēmeion*, which means: that by which a person or a thing is distinguished from others and is known. In other words, signs (from a biblical standpoint) distinguish us from others. Jesus was set apart through the signs that were wrought by His hands. Secondly, the Bible speaks of miracles. What are miracles? The word *miracle* actually comes from the Greek word *dynamis* (du-na-mis), which means: inherent power, power residing in a thing by virtue of its nature, or which a person or thing exerts and puts forth. This is supernatural power that overrides the process of nature. Jesus performed His first miracle at the wedding in Cana (see John 2:1-11). There He transformed water into wine! I would love to have been at that wedding! By turning the water into wine, He bypassed the natural realm and released the supernatural into manifestation. I believe that this is prophetic symbolism of the body of Christ. In John 2:5, the Bible records: "His mother saith unto the servants, Whatsoever he saith unto you, do it." The first key to experiencing the miraculous in our lives is obeying Jesus. Jesus is the Living Word of God, and by obeying the Word of God, we are positioning ourselves to experience His supernatural power (including divine healing).

> *Every believer has been given the power and responsibility to walk in the miraculous.*

The third aspect is wonders! What is a wonder? The word *wonder* comes from the Greek word *teras,* which means: a prodigy. A prodigy is defined as an impressive or outstanding example of a particular person or quality. I believe that as ambassadors of Christ we should be examples of what heaven looks like. Imagine walking in the grocery store and seeing a person in a wheelchair and telling that person to rise up in Jesus' name. Every time we operate in signs and wonders, we get the attention of the unbeliever. Now, this doesn't mean that we should run behind signs and wonders, but it does mean that the miraculous should be evident if we are following the example of Jesus. I believe that the church is in desperate need of an overhaul. If Jesus said that we ought to do greater works than He did, then we should be about our Father's business. Before we can get to the greater works, we need to do the works that He did. Jesus healed the sick. Jesus cast out devils. Jesus cleansed the lepers. This is a great starting place if you want to experience the miraculous in your life. You have to step out on faith and do what the Word of God has commanded you to do!

THE NEW WINE GENERATION

I believe we are living in the last days, and as such, I believe that it is critical for the body of Christ to have a biblical view of her responsibility in the earth. Oftentimes, we hear people talking about the imminent destruction of society or the cultural decay we are facing as a nation, but how often do we hear messages that encourage us to do something about it? Jesus took twelve misfits and turned the world upside down. I believe that this generation will experience and perform greater miracles than any other generation before it. I call this generation the "New Wine" generation. In the book of John chapter 2, the Bible records:

> And the third day there was a marriage in Cana of Galilee; and the mother of Jesus was there: And both Jesus was called, and his disciples, to the marriage. And when they wanted wine, the mother of Jesus saith unto him, They have no wine. Jesus saith unto her, Woman, what have I to do with thee? mine hour is not yet come. His mother saith unto the servants, Whatsoever he saith unto you, do it. And there were set there six waterpots of stone, after the manner of the purifying of the Jews, containing two or three firkins apiece. Jesus saith unto them, Fill the waterpots with water. And they filled them up to the brim. And he saith unto them, Draw out now, and bear unto the governor of the feast. And they bare it. When the ruler of the feast had tasted the water that was made wine,

and knew not whence it was: (but the servants which drew the water knew;) *the governor of the feast called the bridegroom,* (John 2:1-9)

This gospel account is a prophetic illustration of the body of Christ in these last days. Jesus told the servants to fill the six water pots of stone. The bible says that they filled the water pots to the brim. If we want to experience the miraculous power of God we must be filled with the Holy Spirit, who is the agent of the supernatural. Jesus told them to "Draw out now". The expression "draw out" implies pumping from a well, or baling out water. The scriptures declare, "He that believeth on me, as the scripture hath said, out of his belly shall flow rivers of living water." There is a river of the miraculous that flows on the inside of every Spirit-filled believer, but we must draw from that well if we want to experience the supernatural. There is a well of healing on the inside of you right now! Now is the time to draw it out. This is the hour of miracles. You don't need a special degree, position, or designation; all you need is the courage to act on the Words of Jesus. "Draw out now!"

BIRTHING THE MIRACULOUS

I was not always a person who experienced miracles in my life. One day, I became disillusioned with church as usual. I remember saying to God, "There must be more than this!" I was correct! The purpose of this book is to stir up zeal and a passion on the inside of you for more. The Christian life is about more than Sunday sermons and

Bible studies (though these are necessary); we must begin to walk out the Word of God in our daily lives. One day I was preaching a revival service in California. There was a large crowd of people who were anticipating a miracle. During one of the meetings, a lady was brought to the front that couldn't walk. She was born with cerebral palsy, and had suffered from this debilitating illness for years. She saw me on television and the Lord told her that she needed to come to the meeting. She drove over 200 miles to attend. As she came to the front, the Lord told me to tell her to let go of bitterness (remember, Mary told the servants to do whatever Jesus said), so I did just that! Once she heard those words, she began to weep, and I knew (by the Spirit of God) that she had received her miracle in that moment. I told her that she didn't need her walker anymore and I took it out of her hand. Her ankle bones received strength and she began to walk, then she began to run. To God is the glory! This woman was healed in Jesus' name! This is just one of countless miracles that I witness on a regular basis. However, there is so much more! I believe that God is waiting on us to give birth to something greater. You are in the labor room of the Spirit of God, and now it is time to push into the miraculous like never before. I declare that you will experience the accelerated manifestation of God's blessings, grace, and goodness in your life. I declare that you are the head and not the tail, that you are above only and not beneath. You are blessed everywhere you go, because the blessing of Abraham pursues and overtakes you in Jesus name!

PRAYER

Father, in the name of Jesus, I thank you for who you are and all that you have done. Today I declare with bold confidence that I was born for the miraculous. Signs, wonders, and miracles are commonplace because the Spirit of God dwells on the inside of me. Your Word declares that I will do greater works than Jesus according to John 14:12, therefore; I declare that I walk in the supernatural power of God in every area of my life. I possess the miracle anointing inside my inner being. I am a part of the New Wine generation and my life reflects the glory of God. I will heal the sick, raise the dead, and cast out devils according to Mark 16. Fear will no longer limit or control me, because I have the God kind of faith that enables me to do the impossible and experience the miraculous in my life. Thank you for your unlimited power at work in me now! In Jesus' name. Amen!

ABOUT KYNAN T. BRIDGES

KYNAN T. BRIDGES is senior pastor of Grace and Peace Global Fellowship in Tampa, Florida, which reaches thousands of people every week with the gospel. He is the author of the bestselling books *Possessing Your Healing* and *Supernatural Favor*, an international conference speaker, and chairman of the International Apostolic and Prophetic Council (IAPC). His television program, *Life More Abundantly*, reaches millions of viewers every week.